HUNGARIAN FOLK ART
Editor: Gyula Ortutay

Contents

HUNGARIAN
PEASANT
COSTUMES

by Alice Gáborján

Corvina

Title of the Hungarian original: Magyar népviseletek, Corvina Kiadó, Budapest
Translated by Mária Kresz
Translation revised by Caroline Bodóczky
Photos by Károly Koffán
Except II, VII, 5, 21, 23 by Tibor Gyerkó
IX and cover photograph by Károly Szelényi
XV by Attila Mudrák
2, 20 by Kata Kálmán
11 by Domokos Moldován
22, 26, 27 by Ede Tomori
24, 29, 31 by József Fischer
Cover design by Julianna Rácz
Illustrations by Zsolt Csalog
Map by János Lengyel
© Gáborján Alice, 1988
ISBN 963 13 2832 5
ISSN 0324-7996
Second, revised edition
CO 2770-h-8892

Printed in Hungary, 1988
Kner Printing House, Gyomaendrőd

THE DEVELOPMENT OF PEASANT COSTUMES

The definition of popular costume is by no means simple. Socially the concept largely belongs to the sphere of the peasantry.

The development of peasant costumes—just as that of clothing in general—depends on two factors: the human factor and the historical influence. Garments always represent the personal conditions of life; the material and social position of a man; poverty or wealth; youth or old age; and even emotional conditions: joy, grief, or mourning. This is the human factor.

However, the forms of clothing have their historical development. Whatever emotional conditions are represented by garments, they can only be shown within the fashions and the society of the day. This is valid for clothing in general, and it is very true for peasant costumes, which have also evolved within the dual possibilities of personal and impersonal character, the human factor with its emotions, and history with its laws of the society of a certain period.

Interest in folklore began all over Europe in the Romantic age, and with folklore an interest in peasant costumes sprang up. This was the time when intellectuals were amazed by the beauty of folk poetry. And with the newly discovered wealth of rural life came the discovery of peasant attire. It was in this period that illustrated albums and descriptions of popular costumes were published, and the interest of scholars was aroused towards the garments of rural communities still living under feudal conditions.

This initial interest was highly romantic: peasant life being observed only superficially from outside. It was felt that poverty, cultural backwardness, social depression and isolation gave an original and noble simplicity to the lives of the peasants, with their beautiful, gaily coloured clothes and the precise aesthetic quality of every aspect of their everyday life, mirrored in the folktales, songs and woodcarvings. Observers perceived an aesthetic instinct in their colourful, naive costumes, and a moral instinct in their social position. According to this concept, peasant costumes gave the illusion of a good, constant, unchangeable world. From this superficial view, peasants were the embodiment of the natural, happy state, innocence and ancient simplicity.

5

In reality, however, the truth was that the majority of the peasants lived in very miserable circumstances, socially at the bottom of the feudal stratification, retarded in education. As, in the course of history, the lot of the Hungarian people as a whole improved or declined, so the life of the peasant was also somewhat ameliorated or became even harder.

Each historical period was reflected in the clothing of the peasants, in the form of single elements of style. Just as the ever receding ripples made by stone falling into the water are nevertheless still part of that same water, so peasant costumes evolving far from high society and much later than urban fashion, are still a part of the main stream of their culture. Elements of the styles of a particular age may be found, like a distant echo, in the clothes of the peasants, adapted according to their means and way of life. The further away the historical style created by a society in a higher financial and cultural position, the greater the number of variations in the peasant costumes. The relationship between the higher culture, unified within each period, and the peasant culture, developing within it, was balanced by simplicity and the variations created by distance.

As the history of peasant costume has been studied only since the beginning of the last century, little is known from earlier ages. Yet the author will try to sketch the outlines of the history of Hungarian peasant clothing. This survey will concentrate on three main areas: the material of the garments, their colour-scheme, and the system of their cut. Attention will also be given to the number of garments pertaining to one attire and to the time it takes for peasant fashion to change.

Effects coming both from the East and the West have influenced the clothing of the Hungarians ever since their settlement in the Carpathian Basin. From geographical and ethnographical points of view the Hungarian people are a bond between the East and the West. It seems probable that the eastern style of clothing of the Hungarians at the time of the Conquest (AD 896) was highly colourful, and cut in straight lines, in the usual eastern manner.

The lines of cut follow the warp and the weft, and it is these lines that characterize the clothes made out of woven material in the early phases of development. The reason for this is that every little crap of homespun and home-woven flax or hemp linen was very valuable, as so much time was invested in growing, preparing, spinning and weaving it. By tailoring the material along straight lines, each part of the cloth could be placed close to the next, and none of the precious stuff was wasted. Another advantage of cutting along straight or rectangular lines was that the tailoring could be done with less knowledge of craftsmanship.

The original eastern style of clothing of the Hungarians who had already settled in the Carpathian Basin was kept alive by influences of newer migrations coming from the East: the Pechenges, the Cumans, the Jasians. Though little is known of the medieval clothing of the Hungarian peasants, it is assumed that the characteristics of the earlier eastern style were intermingled with the western influences as far as the material, cut, colour and decoration are concerned. It was, no doubt, influenced by the compulsory grey, woollen everyday dress of the medieval European peasant, although the vivid colours of the Gothic age must also have had their effect. Hungarian fashions were strongly influenced by the last great eastern wave of Osman Turks occupying Hungary between the 16th and 17th centuries. This period again saw a colourfulness in clothing and a partial return to the eastern cut. The costumes of this period can be seen in contemporary illustrations of peasants, and on coats of arms. The control of prices at this time suggests that the peasants were already purchasing dyed cloth made in manufactures.

After the Turkish occupation, in the 18th century, the Habsburg empire reorganized the feudal system, and the majority of Hungarian peasants were thrown into a state of still greater misery. But at the same time the influence of western attire again became stronger. The poverty of the 18th century meant that the peasants once again did not have the means to buy the manufactured textiles, and were restricted to self-sufficiency. Agriculture supplied hemp and flax, and animal husbandry sheepskin and leather. Linen was mostly homespun, and rough wollen cloth was woven either by artisans or at home.

At the beginning of the 19th century the clothes of peasants were still largely made of linen, of rough cloth and sheepskin. Textiles made by large-scale industry were increasingly used, though in small quantity. Whilst linen garments made out of rough cloth were fashioned according to the older cut with its straight lines, the upper garments, sewn out of factory-made material, were mostly tailored in western fashion with curved lines of cut.

At the same time the clothing of the upper classes reflected a western orientation, as the country was now part of the Habsburg Empire. As usual, this influence eventually filtered down to the peasants in a modified form.

The needy conditions of the peasantry at the beginning of the 18th century meant a decline not only in material, but also in colouring. Most of the garments were made of homespun linen with its unbleached whitish-yellow colour, out of rough woollen frieze, of a natural white, grey or brown, or of slightly bleached sheepskin. Thus peasants' attire was characterized by the natural white or greyish-brown colours. The bleached and drab decolouration suited the impoverished state of the peasantry. Naturally, this colour-scheme was mainly worn by the poorer class in their everyday vestments, and better-to-do farmers in their work-day clothes, whilst the garments of young people, and especially the finery of richer peasants were as colourful and ornamented as possible.

Even at the beginning of the 19th century, the peasants were wearing clothes made of homespun linen, and in some places used homespun wool, as well as fur and leather from their own animals. These rough home-made clothes retained the old style of straight cut tailoring for a good many years. A slowly increasing number of garments were made of industrially produced material, and cut on the shapely curving lines of western fashion.

Multi-coloured materials were first used for upper garments. In illustrations from the beginning of the 19th century peasant women are to be seen in white petticoats, men in white linen pantaloons, whose upper garments are of dyed factory-made material: on the woman a gaily coloured bodice, jacket, or shawl, on the man a blue cloth vest or waistcoat. Light or dark blue cloth suits become frequent among peasants following the 18th century fashion of the noblemen.

As living conditions somewhat improved in the course of the 19th century, the new prosperity was reflected in the folk costumes, and the former gay colours, especially the hues of red were revived. Dress became vivid in colour and ornamented in detail.

The number of garments composing one outfit were few at the beginning of the 19th century, and comprised only the most necessary pieces. Men's wear consisted of a shirt and pantaloons, or 'gatya', made of yellowish-white linen or hemp, white or grey breeches, a grey, brown or white frieze-coat, a natural sheepskin jacket, 'ködmön', and the 'suba', a sleeveless, almost circular cloak. From the end of the 19th century onwards, sheepskin was increasingly dyed brown. Black boots or sandals completed the men's outfit. Women wore a shirt made of yellowish-white hemp or linen, later of white cambric, a linen skirt and apron, either white or dyed black with oak-apples, an off-white fur-lined 'ködmön', and possibly a sort of rough off-white woollen coat. This was worn with a multi-coloured kerchief and black sandals or yellow, red or black boots.

It is interesting to note the order in which the clothing made of industrial, dyed material first made its appearance in peasant costumes. To begin with, the peasants made garments for the upper body from these new materials. Numerous drawings and paintings from the beginning of the last century show women dressed in white linen skirts with jackets and kerchiefs made of gaily coloured material. The men are seen wearing white linen shirts and pantaloons with blue or black cloth waistcoats and jackets—the influence of the light and dark blue cloth of the garments of the upper classes.

From this it is clear that the peasant costumes did not evolve all at once or remain unchanged. On the contrary, they were continuously changing, though very gradually, in all aspects: material, colour, cut and decoration.

The time it took peasant fashions to change was still comparatively slow at the beginning of the 19th century. The precious garments, which took so long to make, had to remain durable. Peasants had neither the possibility nor the impulse to accelerate the change of fashion.

Thus at the beginning of the 19th century folk costumes were still largely made of material acquired from agriculture and animal husbandry. The system of cut was straight-lined, the colour-scheme white, and decoration was sparse, and mostly red. The attire was composed of few pieces, and fashions changed very slowly.

In the middle of the 19th century, however, great changes took place in the social, economic and educational condition of the peasants, which affected the clothing. As a result of the channelling of the rivers, fertile acreage was liberated from the marshes, and an agricultural prosperity began, which lasted three decades. As well as this, the building of a network of railways also contributed to the sudden rise in the position of the peasantry. Feudal self-sufficiency was followed by the production of commodities and naturally this change had its effect on clothing.

The improved economic condition made it possible to purchase materials made by large-scale industry, and the use of shiny bluish-white cambric, printed cottons and woollen cloth became more general.

The new industrial material not only meant the introduction of colour, but also a gradual change in the cut. The fine cambric was wider than the homespun linen, and the extra width was gathered around the body in pleats. Both men's and women's shirts became gathered, as well as the women's skirts and the men's pantaloons. Garments made out of the colourful, industrial material were also the bearers of the new fashion: curved lines of tailoring. Through these garments came the influence of the contemporary or slightly outdated clothing of the upper and middle classes.

The colour-scheme of peasant costume also changed through the increased use of new materials. Factory-made cambric was white, too, yet compared to homespun bleached linen it was a shiny bluish-white. As a novelty it became a fashion amongst the young and the rich, and its white became the expression of youth, festive occasions and wealth. At the same time the bleached yellowish-white of homespun linen remained the colour of working-clothes, the garb of the poor and the old, a symbol of weekdays with its labour, of poverty and old age. Bleached white was also used for mourning, as in a few places women mourned in white; in other places the dead were dressed and buried in white. The small white bonnet of elderly women also points to the symbolic meaning of the colour. From the social and human points of view bleached white linen gained a negative meaning.

With the introduction of factory-made textiles, not only snow-white cambric, but also the use of many kinds of coloured cottons gained ground. Thus it became possible to make a choice, and clothing became all the more colourful.

Another novelty was the use of black, which came into fashion among Hungarian peasants only in the 19th century, mainly in the second half, and in some places only towards the end of the century. At first black was used for festive appearance and had nothing to do with mourning. Indeed it ranked with red as a festive colour, sometimes even outstripping it as the height of fashion. In the fashion of the upper and middle classes, black had a double meaning: it was used both for great festive occassions and for mourning. Peasants firts used black as a festive attire, and it was only later and gradually used for mourning.

A few examples of the use of both black and red as festive colours: in Szalonta and Várad, the leaves of the red flowers on the cloaks became black; the Palóc people also edged the contours of the flowers on their cloaks in black, and this could be found in Transdanubia, too. The embroidery on the cloaks of the Matyó in Borsod county changed from red to black. This change to black embroidery marked the end of decoration on these cloaks. Nothing followed the black embroidery—the decorated 'szűr', or cloak, simply disappeared. The 'párta' or headdress of the girls in Baranya and Déva used to be red, but after 1887 the red decorative parts of the 'párta' became black in the Sárköz. Girls in mourning did not wear a 'párta'. Black also became the colour for the bride's dress in various parts of the country, such as Mezőkövesd and the country around Kalocsa-Szatmár.

There are many instances from the second half of the 19th century that black, becoming increasingly more fashionable, belonged primarily to the wardrobe of young people. Young men wore a black kerchief around their neck, and details on the headwear of young girls, as well as the coifs of young married women, were black. In some places even the costume of the bride was black. The most decorative period is from the time a girl reaches marriageable age to the birth of the first child. Black appearing at this period therefore points to its being primarily a vogue of fashion, and only secondarily the sign of old age and mourning. In the course of life the red of youth was gradually replaced by blue and green, finally fading to white as life progressed towards old age, and towards mourning. After black had come into fashion for the young, old age and mourning was represented by dark colours.

For the men's costume dark blue cloth became more general, and towards the end of the 19th century, black cloth was the usual material of men's suits.

The costumes of the young women were characterized by the increasing number of garments worn at once, and by their vivid colours. Older women had at first worn green or blue for half-mourning, but this changed first to off-white, then to brown and black, and as the colours darkened so the number of garments worn together grew fewer. Thus as they aged and wore darker and darker clothes, the women became increasingly thinner.

The speed of the change of fashion also grew, but compared with urban fashions it was still very slow.

The new period of development in costume commenced in the second half of the 19th century. It was characterized by a wealth of new materials and colours, by curved lines of cut, an increase in the number of garments worn together, and an acceleration in the change of fashion. Costumes known from that time, and those still worn in the 20th century, evolved within the realm of these factors.

THE AESTHETICS OF PEASANT COSTUMES

Costume is not only the clothing of peasants but is also an aesthetic and psychological mode of expression. Hard peasant life with its everyday labour gives comparatively few opportunities for expressing aesthetic ideals, but costume is one of the few.

Peasant life differs from that of higher levels of society and from urban life. A peasant has a different outlook. So it is natural that the aesthetics evolved in peasant society differ in their details from the aesthetics of the socially more elevated classes.

Even in the 19th century, Hungarian peasant costume was not independent of the fashions of the nobility and the urban bourgeoisie. These classes were in a better position, not only financially, but also culturally, whilst peasants could only gain visual impressions from ready-made fashions. It took time for the details of urban fashions to reach peasant society descending the ladder of rank. So the elements of style coming from 'high' culture always reached the peasants somewhat late.

It was ready-made forms that were adopted by the peasants from the attire of the higher classes, but the whole style never reached them, only certain single elements. The whole construction of the style of the costume had become disintegrated by the time it reached the peasantry, having passed the various classes and strata of society. Thus when talking of Hungarian peasant costumes one cannot speak of costumes of the Hungarian Renaissance, of the period of the Turkish occupation or Baroque or Biedermeyer costume, but one can certainly speak of elements in Hungarian peasant costume deriving from the Renaissance, the Turkish occupation, and from the Baroque or the Biedermeyer styles.

Peasants living in small communities, according to its laws, always alter the elements of style to their own way of life, cultural position, and rules of aesthetics. Their costume is a combination of various styles from different ages, not exactly like any previous style. The main characteristics of peasant aesthetics are therefore not the simple adaptation of elements coming from higher culture, but the reconception or recreation of these into a new unit, differing from the original.

The style of fashions in high culture is marked by contemporary elements. As the style descends and its construction becomes disintegrated, certain elements become linked with others from other periods. By the time it reaches the peasantry, the former unity of the elements has almost completely dissolved. One might say each element represents a period or a style; a new style is born from the fragments: a peasant style.

The dressing of women's hair by parting it in a T-shape, as done in the village of Hollókő, comes from the fashion of the Biedermeyer, whilst rolling the hair from the forehead upward is a belated effect of the 17th-century fashion. The old Hungarian shift, gathered around the neck, has its predecessor in Renaissance fashion, whilst the bodice worn with the shift points to the Baroque. Boots stitched at the side are reminiscent of the Turkish occupation of the 16th and 17th centuries.

It is easier for peasants to integrate single elements than the whole style. There are examples when the composition of the whole is aesthetically less satisfying, yet the details of the costume are pleasant and pretty. For instance, in Hollókő, a kerchief is bound over the coif of young women and is tied at the nape. This kerchief was gradually tied higher and higher, so that the coif had to be drawn down over the forehead, leaving a large portion of it visible at the sides. Around the turn of the century this part of the coif became decorated with coloured frills, and later on, after the First World War, coloured beads were sewn between the frills. Today various patterns are formed out of these beads and they are sewn on white linen bands. These patterns give more aesthetic pleasure to the urban eye than the unusual line of the kerchief, drawn down over the forehead and bound high at the nape. Thus the details may be more pleasing than the whole.

One of the determining factors in the aesthetics of peasant costume is physical work, which is the basis of peasant life. It is natural that the manifestations of people engaged in heavy labour are clumsy and cumbersome. Movements become unwieldy but powerful, and so artistic execution becomes powerful too. The figure of women seems strong and forceful through the increasing number of skirts. It is interesting to note, that whilst strongly stressing the line of the hip, the upper body remains comparatively unemphasized. Strength, based on the robustness caused by physical labour, becomes an artistic quality of peasant composition. With this force, which is sometimes monumental, peasant art attains that aesthetic balance and value through which peasant costume with all its details rises to the height of the aesthetics of the upper classes of society.

Besides hard physical labour, what was the effect of poverty on the costume of peasants? First of all, the time it took to prepare the clothes. The material of homespun garments—hemp and more rarely flax—was grown by the peasants themselves. The seeds were sown by the peasant woman; she pulled the hemp and worked it into thread, and in the winter from early down till late at night she spun it and wove the linen, finally sewing the shirts, the skirts and the pantaloons and embroidering them herself. The often repeated work and her close relationship with the articles resulted in a certain harmony in the order of the details, the arrangement of space and the dynamics of colour, which reached a high aesthetic quality.

Poverty, both material and cultural, resulted in a tendency for stability and rigidity. The bows of ribbons and bonnets were often lined with paper to make them stiffer, so that they would not need rebinding. Peasants avoid lax and temporary solutions and endeavour to find final, solid and stable forms. The kerchief worn in Hollókő is taken off the head without unbinding it, so that next time it can be put on as a complete headdress. Variation and the love for variety is valid only within certain limits. This is one of the ways in which the peasants' feeling for tradition is manifested.

A characteristic tendency of Hungarian peasant art is to crowd the decoration. Sparse decoration is in the eyes of peasants a sign of poverty, whilst a surface well covered is a sign of wealth. The old meaning of the Hungarian word 'paraszt' i.e. peasant, also meant undecorated, plain. Their own labour and time was seemingly free of charge and so the simple homemade clothes could be enriched by embroidery. As the economic position of the peasants improved, it became possible to make even more elaborate embroidery on the surfaces left for decoration, until it became crammed, and finally the design was lost in the endeavour to completely cover the surface with embroidery.

Later it was not the rhythm of the design which remained visible but the rhythm of colour patches. A good example of this is the history of the embroidery on the 'szűr', the famous Hungarian embroidered frieze-coat. The early naturalistic and sparse flower design became increasingly crowded until finally it was impossible to see single motifs, but only the rhythm of colour. The same thing happened to the embroidery of bonnets and other pieces of attire. This tendency is also apparent in the way garments of different colours are worn together.

As a result of the improved economic conditions of the 19th century, more articles were made of factory-made material. Garments became wider and were gathered into folds. The number of skirts and kerchiefs grew, and the headdress was composed of more pieces. The whole attire of a costume was composed of a greater number of garments. The endeavour to express means and resources was not only shown by embroidery and decoration, but also by using as much material as possible.

Colour can also express positive or negative conditions and feelings, both socially and personally. Colours expressing youth, joy and, to a certain extent, richness, are close to one another. Hungarian peasants are very fond of vivid, pure colours, especially red. In the 19th century girls and young women wore red for festive attire, as the symbol of youth and joy. Similarly, dull colours—originally off-white, then grey, brown and other dark colours—suggested age, mourning, and to a certain extent, the daily grind and poverty.

THE ELEMENTS OF PEASANT COSTUMES

The essential traits of peasant garments and hair styles are basically the same all over the country, though deviations of form appear in various regions and at different periods. A general detailed description will be given of the formal elements, followed by the description of the costumes of the different regions.

At the beginning of the 19th century men wore long hair which was tucked up or braided. Young men occasionally had short hair, which was called 'hair cut-in-a-bowl' as a bowl was put on the head in order to cut the hair straight. Long hair went out of fashion around 1848, when the young men called to military service in the War of Indepencence, were obliged to have their hair cut short.

Moustaches were very popular, with the ends twisted into whiskers.

At that time men wore high-felt caps, which were replaced around 1820–1830 by hats with large rims. Low hats with small round rims were also favoured as well as a kind of top hat. A plume was often stuck into the rim. Straw hats were worn for work.

Men's hairstyle, 1900

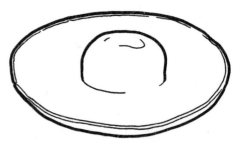

Hat from the Great Pain, 1900

The shirt worn by men had a rectangular front and back, and the sleeves were also made out of rectangles. It had no collar and the opening was tied with tape. The sleeves had no cuffs. In the 18th century and at the beginning of the 19th century the shirt was long and was worn over the trousers, girded by a wide leather belt. Around the beginning of the 18th century a shirt with a very short waist became very popular despite orders forbidding it which were issued until the middle of the 19th century.

A few shirts have survived from the 17th century belonging to members of the Esterházy family, which show that shirts sewn out of rectangles were also worn by Hungarian gentlemen at that time.

Peasant men wore a black kerchief around the neck with this simple shirt—a fashion harking back to the French Revolution.

Linen pantaloons, called "gatya" were cut out of rectangles in the eastern style. Poorer men used to wear two pantaloons in winter, one over the other.

Later on the pantaloons were made out of broad factory-made cambric and became so wide that they resembled a full-pleated skirt. Shirt sleeves, also made of cambric, became similarly wide. Naturally, this change happened first to the festive wear and Sunday clothes.

Sheepskin garments were originally white in all parts of Hungary, but later on they were dyed (not tanned) a brownish colour. Sheepskin garments will be discussed in detail in the next chapter on the clothes of the Great Hungarian Plain.

High cap from
the Great Plain,
18th century

Hat with
a round rim
from Kapuvár, 1960

17

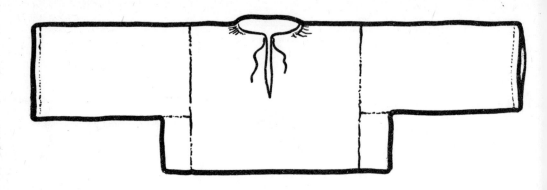

Man's shirt out of rectangular pieces, 1920

Men's footwear included various kinds of laced sandals and, later on, boots. Sandals preceded boots, and herdsmen made them themselves, usually out of untanned leather. The sandals could be worn on either foot. In cold weather the feet were bound with foot-cloths, but in summer sandals were simply worn over the bare foot.

Slippers were worn by men around the house. The toecap and soles were made of tanned leather. In the 19th century slippers were sewn together on the wrong side using a special stitch, and after being softened by dampening, they were turned back to the right side. This method was brought to Hungary by the Turkish army at the time of the occupation.

Boots were much grander and more highly valued than sandals or slippers. High-legged footwear spread among Hungarians in the 16th and 17th centuries, which also points to the Turkish influence. Peasants began wearing boots in the 18th century and at the beginning of the 19th century. The sole was sewn in the same way as the slipper, and the boots could also be worn on either foot. On the Great Plain boots with high heels were popular, especially among herdsmen. The characteristics of Hungarian boots are the side seam, the high front and the method of stitching the sole—all eastern traits. Laced boots, worn only for work, were cheaper, but covered only half the leg.

A very popular garment worn in the last century over the linen shirt and trousers was the 'szűr' as overcoat, made of thick woollen cloth or frieze. In the 18th century the material, especially the finer varieties, was brought from Transylvania.

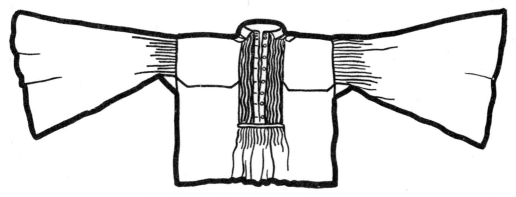

Man's shirt with wide flowing sleeves, 1935

The cut is eastern, and it is made of rectangular pieces. At the beginning of the last century its main decoration was red trimming, and later on, red appliqué; the much admired embroidery with its wide range of colours developed only later. At first the embroidery was naturalistic, representing flowers. According to the laws of peasant aesthetics these became stiffer and more crowded. The effect of the design gradually dissolved and finally only the colour rhythm remained visible in the crowded decoration.

Such an embroidered fancy 'szűr' was naturally primarily a festive garment and also meant that its owner had the means to buy it. Frieze-coats worn for everyday and by poor people remained plain even in the 19th century.

The 'szűr' was worn only by men. Though it had sleeves, they were never used, as it was always thrown over the shoulders and left open in front.

The older type of frieze-coat had a large rectangular collar which could be worn as a hood.

White frieze was used for other garments besides the 'szűr': for the pelisse, the shorter dolman and also the vest. These garments were sometimes trimmed with red. Braided trousers were also made of the same material.

With the industrial revolution in the 19th century, the number of garments made of factory-made material increased mainly, of course, in the wardrobe of richer peasants. Dark blue cloth was especially popular and used for vests at first, and later dolmans, pelisses, and finally trousers. Towards the end of the last century there was a kind of trousers with red trim-

Red boots
from Bács-Bodrog County, 1860–1880

ming and a row of bright brass buttons on the side; blue cloth was replaced by black cloth, although in a few places this change took place later.

The basic elements of women's costumes are to be found all over the country.

Girls wore their hair in a simple plait and used to part it in the middle. Later on hair was parted in a T-shape according to the fashion of the Biedermeyer. The parting line which runs from ear to ear is divided by a shorter parting beginning at the forehead. At first it was fashionable among young girls, but was later adopted by married women. Today it is disappearing as a woman's hair fashion.

On festive occasions girls wore a headdress called 'párta', a wreath of pearls or artificial flowers. The 'párta' was derived from the dress of the higher classes. Married women wore a bonnet or a coif on their knot of hair. In the last century young women wore a 'golden coif' on Sundays later replaced by a bonnet with a white or black frill. A white veil was worn over the coifs.

The shift was made of linen in the Renaissance style, which spread throughout the Hungarian peasant class at the end of the 18th century and the beginning of the 19th century. It was gathered around the collar and had long sleeves, although these later became shorter.

In the course of the 19th century women's linen shifts were sewn of finer cambric, similar to the men's shirts. Often the front and back of the shift were of rougher linen, whilst the sleeves were of cambric. Gradually different kinds of blouses appeared, following the urban pattern; their names are different in every region.

A petticoat made of homespun linen covered the lower body. In the southern territories of Hungary this was sewn out of rectangular pieces, and gathered into folds at the waist. Over the linen petticoat but under the top skirt increasing number of petticoats were worn. In the Great Plain, in the middle of the 19th century, the ideal figure of a robust peasant beauty was attained through wearing many skirts. The festive skirts were made of silk, cashmere, velvet or brocade, the everyday ones naturally being of cheaper stuff.

An apron was always worn over the skirt, and to save material the part covered by the apron was made of cheaper stuff in keeping with the thrifty peasant attidue.

A sheepskin vest or a silk bodice was worn over the shift.

Women wore sheepskin jackets, 'ködmön', similar to those of the men. The cut was the same but it was shorter, and often decorated with appliqué or embroidery, whilst men's sheepskin jackets were left plain.

Besides sheepskin jackets, a kind of coat or pelisse of blue or black cloth with a fox fur collar was worn by women, similar to those of the men. It was called 'mente'.

High boots, a Turkish influence, were also worn by women and were made of red, yellow or later black leather. Even the women wore spurs on their boots, their function was to rattle at dances, and they were different from those worn by men.

FOLK COSTUMES IN THE TERRITORIES INHABITED BY HUNGARIANS

Costumes of the Great Plain

The *Alföld* or Great Plain suffered most grievously during the Turkish occupation in the 16th and 17th centuries. Because of the hostilities and the troublesome times the smaller villages became depopulated and large peasant towns arose.

The fields belonging to these great agrarian towns could only be sufficiently exploited by keeping livestock on them. Large-scale animal husbandry yielded hide and sheepskin, basic raw-materials for clothing. The attire of the herdsmen, though more ancient in style than the clothing of the peasants, was far more ornamented and fanciful.

The peasants of the Great Plain were more conservative in their clothing than their women. In some place men's attire has changed only recently.

The most archaic garb of the herdsmen which occasionally could still be seen after the Second World War consisted simply of two sheepskins, one for the back and one for the front. The skinned natural fell, with the legs left on, was not prepared artificially but only softened. The two sheepskins were worn with the feet tied at the shoulder and at the waist.

A less simple garment was the sleeved sheepskin jacket called 'ködmön' or 'bekecs'. It reached the knees and, in some places, even the ankles. In time it became shorter. It had a standing collar and was trimmed with fur. Such garments were made by furriers, who also did the embroidery.

The first mention of a 'ködmön' worn by a peasant was in 1698, when the mayor of Kecskemét, in the centre of the Great Plain, ordered a shepherd to be caned for wearing a fanciful 'ködmön' and ordered the furrier to undo the decoration and repay the shepherd the difference in price between a plain and an embroidered jacket. It is evident from the severity of the punishment that the fashion for embroidered sheepskin jacket had only recently sprung up among herdsmen. The older type of cut for sheepskin jackets was straight, similar to the clothes made of white frieze, but with the influence of the western way of cutting, this changed into tailoring with curved lines.

A garment most frequently used in the Great Plain was the expensive cloak made out of many sheepskins, the 'suba' or 'bunda'. Depending on the means of the owner, the sheepskin cloak was made out of at least three and a half or four skins but sometimes as many as fifteen. Spread out, the 'suba' forms a complete circle or part of a circle. In Hódmezővásárhely, the cloak was shorter, in the region of Great Cumania and in the counties of Hajdú and Bihar it was longer. Long cloaks reaching to the ground had to be turned up and buttoned in rain or muddy weather. Naturally it was the rich who possessed the wide sheepskin cloak, embroidered by the furrier, whilst the cloak of the poorer peasant herdsmen was narrower, and its leather unprepared, softened by the shepherd himself and left undecorated, in its natural colour.

In very cold weather the men of the Great Plain wore sheepskin breeches with the fur inside. The exterior leather was smeared with lard to impregnate and soften it. Such breeches were worn tucked into the boots, but there were also trousers made of leather which were worn over the top of the boot, buttoning at the side.

At the beginning of the last century herdsmen still wore a wide leather belt called 'tüsző'. It was made out of tanned or smeared horse or cattle hide, and had a pocket in front for money and tools, such as a knife, a flint, steel and tinder for striking fire. Later it was replaced by a narrow belt.

There were different types of frieze-coats, 'szűr', in various parts of the country and the type worn in the Great Plain was the longest. Peasants and herdsmen alike had their 'szűr' but in the eastern part of the Great Plain it was worn only by herdsmen.

In the middle of the last century a new type of 'szűr' appeared in the eastern part of the Great Plain. Besides the large square collar typical everywhere, it had a small standing collar influenced by military uniform and the clothes of the nobility. The decoration of this type of 'szűr' was not embroidery, but appliqué, sewn on by machine. It can be noticed that the lines of cut are slightly curved, in the manner of urban tailoring.

In the eastern, and especially the northeastern corner of the Great Plain a kind of black, or sometimes grey or whitish, overcoat named 'guba' was used. Although it looked like sheepskin, it was in fact material with big tufts of wool woven into it. The weave was not very thick and the 'guba' was a much cheaper garment than the 'szűr' or the sheepskin cloak. Its cut was even simpler than the cut of the frieze-coat, but it was similarly wide and worn thrown over the shoulder. The 'guba' was also worn by women and there was no difference between the one for a man and the one for a woman, in fact in poorer families the husband and wife would only have one between them.

The ancient form of stock-breeding—keeping the stock out of doors almost all year round—was followed longest in two parts of the Great Plain: the Hortobágy (close to Debrecen) and Bugac (close to Kecskemét). In these two regions the old way of life of the herdsmen remained comparatively intact, and with it their old costumes, and some are worn even to this day.

A characteristic of the Hortobágy clothes is that the shirt and pantaloons are dark blue, a reminder that earlier the herdsmen had worn linen impregnated with fat and smeared black. The wide-brimmed hat may still be seen here and also the fancifully embroidered 'szűr', made in Debrecen. An accessory belonging to the equipment of the Hortobágy herdsman before the general use of matches, was a leather case for fire utensils, the steel, flint and tinder.

The herdsmen of Bugac wore white shirts and white 'gatya', pantaloons.

The form of the hat with its high top, which was also worn in the surroundings of Little Cumania, is reminiscent of the earlier high cap, called 'süveg'. Men from these regions can be recognized even today by the big silver buttons on their jackets and vests, buttons similar to those formerly worn by well-to-do peasants and the nobility. Herdsmen's clothes varied according to the kind of animal they tended, and so the horseherd, cattleherd, shepherd or swineherd could be distinguished at a glance.

Contrary to the more conservative men's attire, women's clothes in the Great Plain changed at an early period from peasant costume to fashionable urban dress. The difference between the two sexes is well depicted in a description from 1845 saying that the wife of the countryman appears on the promenade or in church in a modish silken gown with a parasol in her gloved hands, at the side of her husband who is clad in linen pantaloons or blue breeches with his sheepskin cloak over the shoulders.

There are a few data from the territory of the Great Plain regarding the Renaissance shift. In Hódmezővásárhely and its region it was short, hardly reaching to the waist. In Kecskemét the sleeves of the shift were embroidered with silver.

The old costumes were used longest amongst the Hungarians living in the valley of the Black Körös, among the hills of the eastern fringe of the Great Plain. The skirts of the young women were red, whilst elder women wore blue, and the oldest wore black skirts.

Peasant costume with its full skirts may still be seen in two regions of the Great Plain: around Kalocsa, and in Ajak. Not only are many skirts worn one over the other, but they are also rather short.

In Ajak women like to look broad and so put on an amplitude of clothes. A flower-patterned apron is worn over a number of skirts.

The blouse fits the body tightly, and a frilled collar is worn with it. Little girls only wear one frill, and young girls two, although formerly, young girls used to tie as many as three or four frills, one on top of the other.

Nowadays brides marry in white, but not long ago a black kerchief was worn over the shoulders. In Szakmár the dress of the bride is black.

Most of the festive clothes of the women of Kalocsa and Szatmár are white, decorated in many hues of pale colours. The colour-scheme is light and cheerful and the decoration consists of embroidered naturalistic flowers. Such needlework adorns the bonnet, the narrow sleeves of the chemise, the white linen bodice and the white apron, which is trimmed with frill or lace. The full blue or green silk skirt is worn over many petticoats. It is pleated in very small folds and the hem-line is decked with a horizontal row of coloured ribbons. Young girls' hair is decorated with a light blue or pink ribbon tied into a bow in front. Coloured stockings and fine slippers are worn with this festive dress.

Sheepskin cloaks were not only worn by men, but also by women in the Great Plain. These cloaks or pelerines were much shorter than the men's, and could be seen in the last century especially in the district of Great Cumania and in the towns of the Hajdúság.

Costumes of Transdanubia

Western influence had a greater effect in Transdanubia than in other parts of the country. However, traditional peasant costumes were to be found in this region, too, and in some places, in spite of the western influence, their best period was at a later stage than in the Great Plain. Costumes survived longer, especially in the southeastern part of Transdanubia.

The 'süveg', the cylinder-shaped cap, was not quite as high in Transdanubia as in the Great Plain. The swineherd's hat of the Bakony hills resembled the top hat of the early 19th century, but had a round, turned up brim.

Swineherd's hat from the Bakony hills, 1860

At the beginning of the century this brim was broad but in the second half of the century it became narrower. A very low brimmed hat of this type is still worn today in Kapuvár.

At the beginning of the 19th century men's shirts were long, and in the district of the Sárköz they were worn outside the trousers. Shirts with a very short waist were worn, too. Later the waist again became longer, and the shirt was worn tucked into the trousers. The sleeves ended in cuffs. The shirt had either a standing collar or a double collar, and the front was often richly embroidered. Pantaloons or 'gatya', made of homespun linen were worn all over Transdanubia, too.

A black kerchief at the neck was very fashionable. It is certain that black, in this case, did not mean mourning, as the men of Ormánság when in mourning used to wear a white kerchief instead.

The cut of the frieze-coat—the 'szűr'—is about the same in Transdanubia as in the Great Plain, but its proportions are different. The Transdanubian 'szűr' is the shortest of all, but has the largest collar. Its sleeves are short and 'degenerated', ending in a sewn rounded piece of cloth, so that they could not be worn but only used as a pocket, in which the herdsman kept his tools. The swineherds of the Bakony and Somogy forests wore the Transdanubian type of 'szűr' for the longest time.

A frieze-vest and a short jacket or dolman of the same material were worn under the frieze-coat and over the shirt. These garments were trimmed with red cloth and sometimes embroidered.

A simple and singular article is the sheepskin vest worn in Göcsej, which covers only the chest and the sides, leaving the back uncovered but crossed by two straps.

Sheepskin jackets, or 'ködmön', were worn in southern Transdanubia until recently. The sheepskin cloak was also known. These articles in the Sárköz region were decorated with appliqué and embroidery.

Sandals were the most general footwear. Laced boots were worn for work in the area of Sopron, Kapuvár and in the county of Zala. The top was cut out of one piece of leather with only a small backstay added at the inner and outer sides of the ankle. This ingenious cut is of medieval origin. Boots were considered festive and expensive, and were especially popular with high heels. Another boot-like shoe, called 'saru', was also worn. It was not made in the eastern fashion, but sewn with a western technique.

Manufactured cloth came into fashion in the course of the 19th century, first for the vest and a short jacket. At that time, blue cloth breeches were worn only by richer peasants and only for festive occasions. At first the cloth garments were light blue, but later dark blue. The fashion of blue cloth reached the Hungarians living in Slavonia (Yugoslavia) only around 1910. Herdsmen in the district of Göcsej and Hetés wore wide trousers with buttons on the side up till the end of the last century.

One of the most brilliant costumes was that of the women of Sárköz, gorgeous in material, form and colour, and marked by a distinct taste for proportion and quality.

The district of the Sárköz, beside the Danube, was full of swamps and marshes in the last century, with little acreage and needy population. As a result of the draining works in the middle of the 19th century a lot of land suddenly became arable, and yielded an incredible amount of crops. The financial condition of the inhabitants improved in a very short time, and it became possible for them to purchase all kinds of material and clothing. The tailoring of garments changed slowly, but their material as well as the decoration became increasingly lavish.

The 'párta', or beaded wreath, worn by the young girls in the Sárköz, was a hoop covered with red material with five or seven small cones pointing outwards. Around 1890 a new kind of 'párta' came into fashion which consisted of three pieces, the lower two bands covered with the fashionable black and only the top band covered with red.

The hair of the married women was parted in the middle and two small knots were formed on either side. A coif or bonnet covered the hair in the front. If the hair was too thick some of it was cut off.

The coif was made out of a piece of rectangular black muslin. Later it was made of black silk or cotton, and its shape changed to an oblong. The Sárköz coifs were embroidered with the finest needlework, stitched with white thread representing artistically stylized flowers. These coifs are the pride of Hungarian museums and are a proof of the excellent taste of Sárköz women and their ability to design. The coif was only worn by the young woman for a few years after her marriage, until she was about twenty or twenty-two years old. The black foundation of the embroidery is again a fashion and has nothing to do with mourning.

As was the custom all over Hungary, it was during the years before the first child was born, that the clothing of the young women was the most decorative. In the Sárköz, women would wear a long white veil called 'bibor' over the embroidered coif, the two ends trimmed with a border embroidered with gold or silver passing, and spread on the breast to show the needlework. The veil was fixed on either side of the forehead with three ornate hair-pins. A veil arranged in a similar fashion appears in the 17th and 18th centuries among the costumes of the nobility. The Sárköz headdress was completed by a tassel made of beads hanging from the back of the coif.

The shift was made in the Renaissance style, in the region of the Sárköz, and its material was a remarkably fine homespun crêpe called 'száda', embroidered with crewel-work. The design on the shift differed from that on the coif, which again differed from the border of the veil, thus every kind of garment had an embroidery of its own. The neck of the shift was a frill trimmed with black ribbon and the front of it was covered by beads strung to form a net-like collar.

The lower body was covered with a white skirt of 'száda'. In the Sárköz the skirt was often fourteen yards wide and gathered into many folds. Three or four white petticoats of factory-made cambric were worn over the linen skirt. The top skirt was sewn out of red, blue or green material, and was lined with a contrasting colour at the hem-line. It was customary to tuck up the skirt in front and fix it into the belt so that the lining would show. Later this fashion ceased and the coloured cloth was not sewn on the inside, but on the outside, as a border. The part of the skirt underneath the apron was always made out of a different material.

A bodice was worn over the shift, with a kerchief over it. Later on—in keeping with the peasant tendency for excess—not one, but as many as four kerchiefs were worn one over the other, of which the lowest was the largest. Each of these kerchief was trimmed with a row of silk tassel.

The apron was formerly made of homespun crêpe, but later out of silk or velvet, and was gathered into large folds at the top. White aprons were only worn by very old women. Since 1940 the material of the apron and the skirt has always been the same, and each skirt has an apron to match.

Gradually blouses came into fashion, replacing the shift. These blouses were straight-cut, standing away from the waist, and a chemise with narrow sleeves was worn underneath. The sleeve of the chemise was decorated with beads, and it was girded with a belt.

Embroidered detail of the frieze-coat or 'szűr' from the Bakony hills, 1890

A small short-waisted jacket with a very low-cut front was sometimes worn over the chemise. It was sewn out of black cloth, cotton or silk.

Formerly women wore sheepskin jackets decorated with red leather appliqué and embroidery. The two corners of the jacket were hitched up in front.

Yellow boots in the Turkish fashion were worn at the beginning of the last century for festive occasions but later red boots became popular, and still later the colour of women's boots became black. Embroidered black or green slippers were also worn, and shoes soon became popular. Stockings were knitted out of black wool and more recently knitted stockings with raised bobbles came into fashion.

In the Sárköz, girls and young women preferred red and other vivid colours. As the women grew older, their clothes were made of materials in shades considered as 'mourning colours', such as blue and green. The deepest mourning, however, was white.

If a young girl, who had been confirmed and was therefore considered marriageable, died, she was dressed and buried in bridal clothes. If an old women died, she would be buried in the clothes she had worn as a young woman. Today folk costumes can only be seen on women over forty in the villages of the Sárköz.

The costume of the Ormánság was characterized by white linen, and therefore seemed the most archaic.

The hair of the girls was parted in the middle, a way of hairdressing probably more ancient than the Biedermeyer fashion. The hair was plaited and a red bow was tied at the top and the bottom of the plait. Girls of Ormánság—as well as girls in every part of the country—never wore a coif or a bonnet on their heads. As their hair was very greasy, a bit of trimmed silk was placed beneath the plait to keep the shift clean.

Married women's hair was parted in the same way as the girls', and was plaited into double braids and twisted on the nape. If the hair was too thick, it was thinned. A coif covered with coloured silk and lavishly decorated with artificial flowers, gold and silver threads; broad silk ribbons and black lace was placed on the knot of hair. The form of the coif, the colour-scheme of the decoration and the colouring of the ribbons all indicated the age of the woman. Up to thirty, the main colour was red, and during this period the ribbons were broadest and most vivid. Between thirty and forty, blue, white and green were mixed into the red, and these colours gradually increased until between the ages of forty and fifty the basic colours became blue and white, the coif becoming smaller and its ribbons narrower. After fifty the coif was quite tiny, all white and without a paper stiffening inside, and without any ribbons. But a white coif was also worn by those in mourning.

Pin for fastening
the viel, Sárköz 1925

30

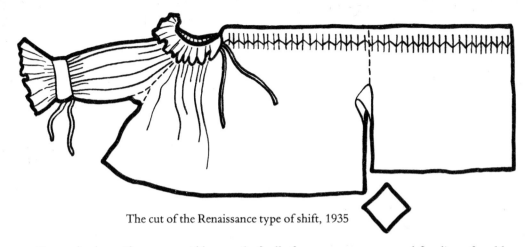

The cut of the Renaissance type of shift, 1935

Formerly the coif was covered by a veil of tulle for young women, and fine linen for older ones, and it was fastened to the hair with a hair-pin.

Women wrapped themselves in a sheet-like covering to protect themselves against rain and cold, dust and mosquitoes.

The shift of young women, expecially the festive shift, was made out of tulle or very fine linen. Under the tulle another chemise was worn which had narrow embroidered sleeves visible through the transparent tulle. Old people, poor people and those in mourning, however, wore a simple unbleached linen shift.

The characteristic skirt called 'bikla' was always white and was made of tulle, fine linen or homespun cambric. Five or six such white skirts could be worn one over the other. Tulle skirts were only worn by the very young. Older women, as well as those in mourning, wore skirts and shifts made out of unbleached yellowish-white homespun cambric.

A singular garment worn over the shift was a vest without a back, fastened together with straps. For young people it was made out of coloured cashmere, whilst the vest of older women was made of unbleached linen.

The aprons of young women were coloured, old women wore white ones.

Around the turn of the century a blouse deriving from the urban fashions of the 19th century became popular. It was made out of silk for festive occasions and for young people, whilst the blouse for everyday wear and for elderly women was made out of blue linen.

31

Very old women used to wear white. When black ceased to be a fashionable colour, it became the colour of age, replacing white. The blouses were wide at the waist-line and worn outside the skirt.

The short white or yellowish sheepskin jacket, or 'ködmön', was decorated with coloured embroidery and trimmed with black lamb. The shape of the 'mente' or pelisse was similar to the 'ködmön', but the material was blue cloth, the collar and cuffs were of red fox skin, and it was braided in front.

In the summer, as well as in rainy weather, women went barefoot. There are data about sandals for women, yet expensive boots were the most popular, and were only worn by women in the Ormánság. These boots were red at first, and black later. A description from 1551 mentions yellow and red boots worn in this territory.

Folk-costumes have rarely been seen in the villages of the Ormánság since the First World War. There are only a few old women who still wear the old garments on weekdays as well as on Sundays.

Most colourful were the silk costumes of Püspökbogád, Egerág and Hosszúhetény. A typical feature in these villages was the way women's hair was dressed by drawing it deeply down to the forehead and rolling it upwards. The hair of married women was pinned up into a bun, which was covered with a coif embroidered in black on a white or red background. Later the coif was made of artificial paper roses and was decorated with small spangles in the shape of half-moons and stars. This coif had a big stiff bow at the back which covered the neck. A kerchief was also worn, red for young women, with a starched white cloth beneath it.

Widows and women in mourning wore a coif of white lace with a white-and-blue decoration. The bow in this case was made of white, blue and green ribbons.

Many skirts were worn, and the skirts were wide. The top one was drawn in by a band to fit the body. It was often made of silk, but the part under the apron was of cheaper material.

The aprons were also of patterned silk with black lace trimming, similar to the kerchiefs worn on the shoulders. The apron could also be drawn in to fit the waist.

The sheepskin jacket—ködmön'—was very short waisted. It was made of white lamb decorated with dark red leather appliqué or with embroidery, and fashionably trimmed with a black border. It was very low cut at the neck.

In the village of Törökkoppány girls wore their hair in a bun. The coif of married women was a brocade kerchief lined with paper.

Embroidery on the veil worn by young women in Sárköz, 1925

The urban blouses of the 19th century replaced the shift at an early period. On holidays an expensive brocade skirt was worn with a big *tournure* underneath. An apron was tied over the skirt. Beads were worn round the neck.

The headdress of the married women of Csököly was similar to the 'párta'. It was covered with black silk for young people, whilst old women and those in mourning covered it with white linen.

The sleeves of the shift were long, and the skirt was white or coloured. Young people wore a coloured apron, whilst the apron of the old and those in mourning was white. Women in mourning and old women covered their heads with a big white cloth.

A sheepskin pelerine similar to the men's sheepskin cloak was worn by married women, whilst young girls had an embroidered sheepskin jacket. Black boots or laced shoes belonged to the outfit. Today all this is vanishing rapidly.

In the district of Göcsej and Hetés young girls and married women rolled their hair upward. This way of dressing the hair is very interesting because it is a combination of the 17th and 18th century upper class fashion of rolling the hair, and the Biedermeyer influence of parting it in a T-shape. A wooden cap covered the knot of hair. The coif made of red rose-patterned material was placed on this and tied with a white ribbon which hung down in front, almost to the waist. Beneath this a black ribbon was tied, but this was only worn until the birth of the first child. Formerly a white starched kerchief folded into rectangle was worn in the sun, to shade the face. This kerchief, called 'pacsa' was still to be seen around 1910 in the region of the river Lendva. Earlier it had been worn by peasants in other regions as well, and is mentioned in a picture-album appearing in 1816 about the counties of Zala, Győr, Vas and Moson.

The shift was replaced by a kind of blouse which young girls wore girded with a shiny leather strap.

The skirt was red or blue, and generally four or five of them were put on together. Earlier a skirt had been worn made of white homespun linen but dyed black. A skirt sewn to the bodice was sometimes worn. The apron, longer than the skirt, was blue for weekdays and black for holidays.

On holidays a white kerchief trimmed with frills was placed over the white shift. If the weather was cool, a kind of blanket was used instead. A yellow sheepskin jacket was also worn.

The clothing of Fadd, Tolna county, has kept many very significant traits of old tradition. A special feature in the costumes of Fadd was the short shift which did not even reach the waist. This variant of the Renaissance shift once general all over Europe was perhaps known in many parts of Hungary. The linen skirt, or 'pendely', which originally matched the short waisted shift, had a high waist-band and two shoulder-straps. Later on a skirt like this was worn over the linen underskirt, which was sewn to the bodice. The border was lined with red and tucked into the waist at both sides so it showed. A kerchief was worn over the bodice and four rows of silvery beads around the neck. Red boots completed the costume.

In cold weather a sheepskin jacket reaching the waist was worn, or a similar jacket made of blue cloth.

The vivid costumes of Sióagárd are still frequently seen. A type of long blouse, trimmed with lace is worn under a silk jacket. The skirt is made of white homespun linen folded into very small pleats, and the flowered apron is also trimmed with lace. The stockings are knitted in a colurful pattern or decorated with white knobs. Flowered slippers are worn on the feet.

In Kapuvár the traditional costumes are still worn, even by some of the men.

The girls' hair is parted in a T-shape or into four divisions, and rolled upwards in front. The married women form their knot of hair simply by combing it back. Formerly, a comb was stuck into the bun and a red kerchief was bound over it. On holidays an ornate coif was worn with a kerchief made out of transparent tulle or white batiste with white embroidery.

A kind of blouse, called 'rékli', replaced the shift at an early period. This blouse is cut to fit the body and is worn outside the skirt. The material is the same as the skirt and may be made out of silk or velvet.

A kerchief is tied over the shoulders under the 'rékli'. It gradually became smaller and at present two are worn at once, one on the shoulders and one round the waist.

The skirt has gradually become shorter, and today it reaches to the middle of the calves.

Coif decorated with spangles, from Kapuvár, 1950

35

It used to be pleated into tiny folds, but today the pleats are flat and big. The skirt is made out of various kinds of brocade, the finest being blue silk or velvet sprayed with a pattern of small shiny stars.

The bodice is made of red, blue or purple velvet, or of brocade with a white background.

A *tournure* is worn sewn to the linen petticoat which is attached to a sort of bodice.

The festive apron is made of iridescent silk, and trimmed with lace and braiding. An apron made of shiny black cotton, which is considered less festive, is worn for going shopping or into town. A white apron is worn at dances with a white kerchief to match on the shoulders.

In the last century seven or eight strings of beads were tied around the neck, but today only three or four are worn.

Boots are mainly worn in the winter, and in the summer red shoes, with two or three straps, are most popular.

Costumes of the Uplands

The Hungarians living in various regions of the Uplands have very varied costumes. These were late in reaching their peak of decoration, and in some villages this was only in the 20th century, though the vine-growing folk of Eger were wearing their characteristic costume, with its many full short skirts, in the middle of the last century.

'Palóc' is the name of a large and important group of Hungarians living in many villages in the Uplands. A smaller group but well-known for its colourful costumes is the 'Matyó'. The villagers along the Galga stream are also known for their costumes. The people of the Uplands were mostly very poor for they hardly made a living out of their scanty land. In the last century, mines were opened in the Palóc region leading to certain financial improvement, and simultaneously the clothing of the peasant women became more lavish. The 'Matyó' folk of Mezőkövesd and its surroundings were either landless, or had very small holdings, and had to leave their homes each year to do seasonal labour, and to harvest in distant states in other parts of the country. These seasonal labourers, men and women, and even young girls and children, were the carriers of fashions and vogues, for they had travelled, seen the world, and seen what other people wore. So it was the poorer, lower strata of society who were the innovators of clothing and brought new elements of dress, preceding the well-to-do peasants. A peasant with means preferred to use the raw materials from his own farm, whilst the seasonal labourer would be readier to spend his (or her) money on clothing. The laboriously earned, miserable pay disappeared on dresses for women, and especially for girls.

Though the Turks did not occupy the whole of the Uplands, certain elements of Turkish origin reached this territory. In 1870 a curious way of wearing the hair was described, the men would have their head shaved leaving only a tassel of hair which then was fastened up is some way. There are also data from the last century showing that the moustache was shaved off completely or was cut shorter. As headwear, men put on high caps, like the one worn in other parts of the country, and later a hat with a large brim came into fashion.

The short-waisted shirt made of homespun (and home-woven) hemp–linen and cut on straight lines was worn in this part of country until a fairly late period. The shirt was matched with linen pantaloons, 'gatya'. In Piliny and Bény the men wore tight breeches. These were made out of hemp–linen and were baggy in front, reminiscent of the 16th-century fashion in Western Europe. Thus Palóc men's fashion included both Turkish fashion of shaving off the hair and the western fashion of breeches.

Workmen also wore aprons, and embroidered ones on Sundays.

Among the garments made of woollen cloth and sheepskin, the frieze-coat or 'szűr' must be mentioned first. The frieze-coat of the Uplands is shorter than that of the Great Plain, but longer than the Transdanubian one, and has little decoration. Homemade cloth was woven from unbleached wool by the Palóc women in the 19th century, and rough cloth breeches were made out of it. The expensive sheepskin cloak was rare in this part of the country, and the 'szűr' was more generally worn. The sheepskin jacket, however, was more common and trousers made of sheepskin could be seen.

Dark blue or black cloth, replacing the frieze and whitish homespun woollen cloth, came into fashion comparatively late, only in the 1890's. At first only the richest peasants owned dark blue cloth breeches, which they wore at their wedding. Later these were lent to the poorer peasants for their wedding.

Sandals—formerly the normal footwear—were only worn by herdsmen and by the poorest by the turn of the century, although they were also worn for harvesting. On weekdays poor people had laced boots whose cut was derived from the Middle Ages. High boots were first only worn on Sundays, and only by the richer villagers, but later they were worn on weekdays, too, and the poorer classes also had them.

In the northern part of the country the costumes of the women were most varied, and in many villages are still worn and even becoming more lavish. It was in this territory that the golden and silver lace adornment of married women's coifs persisted longest and in the most varied forms.

One of the most remarkable groups of the Palóc costume can be seen in Hollókő and the neighbouring villages.

The hair of the women is parted in a T-shape and rolled up in front. A kerchief is always worn over the coif, tied at the back of the neck. It is lined with paper to make it stand stiffly. Another kerchief is bound over it, drawn down on to the forehead, but this one is tied under the chin. The first kerchief leaves only the two sides of the coif visible so it is this part which is decorated. The decoration formerly consisted only of rows of ribbons folded into tiny pleats, but today coloured beads are sewn between the ribbons. The coif is made in light colours for young married women, whilst old women and those in mourning have blue, green or black ones.

The shift is sewn of hemp-linen, but the sleeves are made of finer shop-bought cambric. Until recently, the sleeves of the festive shift and the bride's shift were made of tulle.

Up to ten strings of red or white beads are worn around the neck, with a small heart hanging from the middle string. Older women and those in mourning wear blue or green beads, but the oldest women do not wear beads at all.

The innermost petticoat, 'pendely', made out of hemp-linen is not very wide and is tight at the waist. Three or four, and formerly even more, coloured cotton petticoats were worn over it, and on top of these four or five white petticoats of fine cambric. The top skirt of young women and girls is usually red, patterned with flowers. Brides wear a white batiste skirt above the petticoats. The skirts are usually gathered into small pleats, except the part under the apron which is left unpleated, and is made of cheaper material. The trimming of the skirt is of a vivid colour, the favourite being bright pink.

A sleeveless silk bodice is worn over the shift with a kerchief tied over it. A small piece of coloured material is placed around the neck beneath the kerchief to look like another kerchief.

A short-fitted jacket made out of dark or black material is worn in winter, at Lent and for mourning. Young women wear a brown leather vest on Sundays embroidered with red and green silk yarn and trimmed with red leather.

Two kinds of aprons are worn. One is very wide and almost covers the whole skirt. It is black and is only worn on holidays. When the women are not going to church a narrow apron called 'szakácska' is worn on top of the wide apron. On weekday only the narrow 'szakácska' is worn. It is black, with coloured needlework at the bottom, which is usually blue for old women and women in mourning.

Stockings are worn on Sundays: white ones for young people, blue for the middle-aged, and brown or black ones for old women. Laced sandals were worn here, too, but were later replaced by red and then black boots. The soles of the black boots are nailed according to the western technique, but are sewn at the side in the oriental way. In summer, shoes with double straps are worn on Sundays.

The villages in the northern part of the valley of the Zagyva, especially Kazár, have very picturesque costumes. The headdress of the married women is a combination of the bonnet and the girl's 'párta'. Gold or silver lace or tulle frills adorn this headdress, and long ribbons or patterned bands hang down at the back to the bottom of the skirt. Newly married women tie a white tulle kerchief over it. This headdress is only worn on the greatest holidays.

Brides formerly married in the beaded wreath called 'párta' with a veil attached to it and long ribbons hanging down the back.

At about forty, women stop wearing the festive headdress, and only wear the plain linen bonnet, with a kerchief over it, tied at the back. Unlike the Hollókő kerchief, it is not drawn tightly over the forehead, and as it is not raised at the sides, there is no decoration on the under-bonnet. For the most festive occasions a shift made out of white flowery tulle, with blue starched cambric sleeves beneath the transparent tulle, is worn.

The petticoat worn closest to the body is made out of hemp-linen, and is very narrow. White starched petticoats are worn over it, the innermost being shortest and each successive one a bit longer than the last. Finally comes the top skirt, which is sewn to the sleeveless bodice. This is sometimes lifted in front under the wide apron to show the underskirt. With so many skirts the women look very broad. Only a few old women, between seventy-five and eighty, go to early mass in the sheepskin jacket or the blue cloth' mente' inherited from their mothers. In cold weather, in winter or at Lent younger women wear a short well-fitting jacket, trimmed with a gold or silver lace border.

Boots are still worn, but shoes are becoming increasingly popular.

The costumes of Galgamácsa have a very fresh effect and are still to be seen. The development of peasant costumes reached its peak here only in the 1940s. The young girls have three plaits and a ribbon is bound into each, and tied with a bow at the top and bottom. Women divide their hair crosswise. The girl's headdress, the 'párta', was worn in the last century. The Sunday coif is trimmed with golden lace, and young married women wear a white veil over it. Should a young woman die, she is buried with the coif and the veil.

Beads are worn around the neck and tied at the back with a bow of ribbons.

Today a blouse is usually worn instead of the shift, and is not tucked into the skirt, but worn outside it. When, however, they do wear a shift, a kerchief fringed with tassels is worn over the shoulders. In winter a well-fitting jacket with a warm lining is put on.

Five or six full petticoats are put on over the linen one. Young people wear red top skirts with black edging, whilst older women wear dark blue skirts, edged with red cloth. The red skirts, the blue apron and a coloured kerchief give a most pleasing colour-effect.

In the summer, the women wear shoes, in the winter boots, and for harvest they put on the old-fashioned sandals.

Multicoloured, picturesque clothes are worn only for a short time in life. The colour-scheme becomes darker and after thirty the women only dress in black.

A peculiar style developed in Bény (Biňa) and a few neighbouring villages: the waist of the dress became longer—the longest of all Hungarian peasant costumes—and at the same time the skirt became the shortest. Clothes here are very colourful and the boots are red. Altogether the costume has an unique effect.

The coif of the married women is made out of paper, covered with red material for week-days, and gilt or silver ornaments for Sundays. A bleached and starched tulle kerchief is bound over the coif. Young women wear a band with a bleached frill round their foreheads. As they get older this is replaced by black frill. The kerchief for the head is usually red for the young ones.

The girls wear several strings of beads, with a triple bow of ribbons underneath, and the young women tie coloured ribbons on their sleeves. The workday shift has tight sleeves, and is worn with a red bodice. The Sunday bodice is made of silk or velvet.

Formerly, a large tulle kerchief was worn over the shoulders, and later a silk scarf with tassels around the edge. The silk scarf of old women was black, dark brown or purple.

A cloth jacket with puffed sleeves is worn over the scarf. In winter it is a velvet one lined with sheepskin.

The innermost petticoat is made of either rough hemp-linen or fine factory-made cambric. The unusual silhouette of the Bény women is achieved by tying the petticoats and the skirts below the waist, on the hip, so that the waist appears longer. The inner petticoats are the longest, becoming gradually shorter, and the top skirt is shortest of all. The top skirt is usually red and the trimming is always green. If the skirt is a light colour, the apron must be black, but a white apron is tied over a red or dark skirt.

When going to church a little white handkerchief is held in the hand with the initials and a red or blue flower embroidered in one of the corners.

Until recently young women wore high red boots, which were wrinkled at the ankle. Shoes were laced with red or blue ribbons and thick knit blue stockings with a red pattern were worn to match.

If a young woman died she was buried in her most beautiful dress with a handkerchief in her hands. The coif, however, was not put on and her hair would only be covered with her tulle veil.

The costumes of Martos (Martovce) are especially beautiful. A sudden prosperity sprung up at the turn of the century as the result of the regulation of the rivers, and this prosperity had its effect on the clothing.

Before the First World War the young girls and married women used to wear a black pleated band on their hair, pointed in front and forming two arches over the forehead. The hair of the married women was rolled around a comb to form a bun. This was covered by a coif, which the young women wore decorated with gold and silver lace. The colour of the coif and the silk lace on it was red for young wives, and then, as the women grew older it became blue, green, purple, and finally black. Golden lace was only sewn on to the red coifs. Coloured ribbons hung down from the back. The headdress of young women was occasionally covered with a white batiste or lace shawl. As the women grew older the golden lace and the ribbons gradually disappeared. The back of the old woman's bonnet had the black appliqué embroidery typical of Martos. A kerchief folded into a triangular shape was tied over the bonnet so that the headdress appeared wider at the sides.

Two or three strings of coloured crystal beads were worn, as well as four to six silver chains with a little heart hanging from them.

The sleeves of the shift were often made of fine shop-bought cambric and starched a lighter or darker blue. The sleeves were decorated with red, blue or green appliqué embroidery and ended in ruffles. The high bodice is a comparatively new garment and no kerchief is worn over it. This kind of bodice is not traditional in Martos, and is not put on the dead.

The inner petticoat, 'pendely', of homespun linen, with two shoulder straps used to be worn alone in the summer, as late as 1870–1880. The number of the skirts gradually increased until finally up to five skirts were worn. In time skirts became shorter in Martos, too. The apron was pleated and recently the pleats have become smaller making the apron narrower.

A kerchief is usually worn over the bodice (except for the one mentioned above), but this kind of bodice is deeply cut at the front. The kerchief is decorated with appliqué work and is trimmed with ruffles.

A well-fitting lined jacket is also worn with the bodice and the kerchief, and is made out of red, mauve or black material. The winter jacket is lined with lambskin.

Recently a straight blouse has been worn instead of the shift.

Formerly boots were red, very pointed and the whole top wrinkled. Black boots were more novel and were rounded at the toe. Slippers also used to be worn, but shoes and fashionable sandals are now replacing both boots and slippers.

In Martos black is worn both for festive occasions and for mourning. At church at Christmas, Easter and Whitsuntide black is worn, and also for communion. The colour of half-mourning is blue and green.

One of the best-known peasant dresses in Hungary is the 'Matyó' costume worn by the people of *Mezőkövesd* and two neighbouring villages. This dress has begun to die out recently. While in the Uplands width is the ideal of beauty, in Mezőkövesd women try to achieve a tall slender figure by wearing few but long skirts, a very tight blouse which flattens the breasts, and a conical coif to give an impression of height. The 'párta' used to be worn by the girls here, too. The linen bonnet of married women used to be stuffed in the shape of a hoop. Later a conical coif came into fashion, made of straw, and this coif has become increasingly smaller and more pointed. A bow of ribbons stiffened with paper was placed on it and, finally, the bow took a polygon form. On the top of this coif came a black veil, but this was only worn by very young women before the birth of their first child. Should a women die young, she would be buried in this black veil.

Young women also wear a flower-patterned kerchief tied at the nape. The woollen tassels of this kerchief were at first long and sparse, but later became denser, until today this type of kerchief looks like a lot of pompons. Another type of kerchief was tied under the chin and fixed on a wire frame and was known as the 'tent-like kerchief'.

Three or four strings of blue or red beads—formerly more—were worn. A string of all-white beads was more novel, and a collar made entirely out of beads, similar to the one worn in the Sárköz, was also worn by the 'Matyó' women.

The sleeves of the shift were often made of fine material which was starched. A shift with narrow sleeves and embroidered cuffs was also worn.

The shift was replaced by various kinds of blouses with stiff sleeves, sometimes even lined with paper.

The bodice was either very low-cut or buttoned to the neck. The sheepskin vest was embroidered with coloured silk or wool and decorated with leather appliqué. The blue cloth jacket 'mente' was worn by the 'Matyó' too.

The sheepskin jacket was white and the embroidery was especially beautiful, with a most effective rhythm of colours.

The inner linen petticoat was fashioned so that it was broader at the bottom. The seams were sewn together with needle-point lace, a very old type of lace which was visible on both sides, when the skirt was pinned up in front.

In contrast to the many skirts worn by the 'Palóc' women, the women of Mezőkövesd wore only one skirt at first, and later never more than three or four. The petticoats had a frill round at the hem so the skirts stood out at the bottom, stressing the slender tall figure. When the 'Matyó' costume reached its prime in the 1920s and 30s, the frill was sewn out of over a hundred yards of material. The top skirt was often silk or cashmere, but as the woman grew older her skirts were made out of cheaper and darker material. The top skirt was sewn to the bodice.

The very wide apron, typical of the 'Palóc' costume, was only worn by the bride. The 'Matyó' people, however, had an apron very characteristic of their costume: it was narrow, always made out of black or dark blue cloth, or black velvet, with embroidery at the bottom, to which rows of glittering spangles were later added. The expensive gilt and silver spangles made such huge inroads into the mean wages of the seasonal labourers that the church authorities proclaimed a campaign against the extravagance. As a result the glittering spangles were solemnly burned at the stake in the year 1924. After that they were imitated by yellow embroidery.

The oldest type of footwear were laced sandals, which were followed by slippers and boots. At the beginning of this century black boots came into fashion, instead of the former red ones, and later ready-made shoes and urban sandals became popular.

Black had a festive meaning among the 'Matyó' people, too. Around 1910 brides were married in black. When black became a symbol of mourning—at a much later date amongst the 'Matyó' folk than elsewhere—the bride's dress became colourful again, as it had been before. But since 1927 the 'Matyó' bride has been dressed in white.

If a young girl dies, she is buried in her bridal wreath, as is customary in most parts of the country. The married woman is buried in the coif of her youth, at whatever age she dies.

The costume of the southern villages along the Galga, such as Tura and Boldog, is short-skirted and is a transition to the 'Palóc' costume.

Women rolled the front of their hair upwards in Tura, though now it is either plaited or combed straight back. Formerly the bride wore a 'párta'. The young woman's coif is made of brocade trimmed with golden lace. A white veil used to be worn over the coif for three or four years after the marriage, but later only a kerchief. The newer kind of coif leaves the ears free. In Tura even the old women are buried in their bridal dress.

The inner petticoat is made of hemp-linen and used to hang below the skirt at the back or all around. Since 1910 many petticoats have been worn simultaneously, a fashion innovated in the village by the girls going away for seasonal work. One of the petticoats is made of col-oured flannel with a red edging, and has a pocket. The top skirts are colourful, and for Sun-days they are usually red. It is considered beautiful to be broad at the waist so a *tournure* is worn under the skirts. The apron is very wide and is either white or blue.

A silk or brocade bodice in blue, green, brown or black is worn over the shift, and the back is decorated with black braid or silver passing. Today, a blouse is usually worn instead of the shift.

The sheepskin jacket used to be white or brown with green embroidery, and the one made of blue cloth was lined with lamb and trimmed with fox.

The white kerchief for the shoulders is most delicately embroidered, and needlework also embellishes the handkerchief, carried in the hand to church. Beads are worn until the woman is about fifty years old.

The former laced sandals are now made out of the top part of boots, and are worn only at harvest-time. The favourite footwear used to be high boots, which were red at first, but later black. Shoes were first worn by the Tura peasant women in 1915, and today they are far more usual than boots.

If a woman from Tura marries into another village she does not keep her costume. If, however, a peasant woman from another village marries into Tura she sticks to her own costume throughout her life, but when her daughters grow up she prepares their clothes in Tura style. Around the turn of the century, costumes were even more colourful and the bride married in a multicoloured dress. Later black became fashionable, but this soon became synonymous with old age, and today brides are married in white.

The women of Boldog also roll their hair upward, and make a small knot at the back of the head, on which a little pointed coif is placed with many coloured ribbons hanging down. The kerchief for the shoulders is embellished with open-work embroidery and trimmed with frills. The flower-patterned skirt is pleated into tiny folds.

The Buják costume is characterized by its many short skirts. On holidays the women wear two shifts, one over the other, and adorn themselves with as many as eighteen to twenty rows of white beads. For festive occasions they wear a coloured headband beneath their coif, and above the whole headdress is placed a bunch of coloured blown glass beads on silver and gold threads. Until the Second World War their boots were red, but today they are always black.

Costumes of the Transylvanian Hungarians

The costumes of Transylvania (today part of Romania) are altogether older than those of the Great Plain; one can clearly distinguish certain elements deriving from the 17th and 18th-century fashions of the Transylvanian noble families. Among the Hungarians of Transylvania several groups can be distinguished. The largest group is that of the once privileged Székelys. Another significant group is around Kalotaszeg, comprising the villages west of Kolozsvár (Cluj). Well-known for their costumes are the people of Torockó (Rimetea), the Hungarian villages in the central region of Transylvania, such as Magyarpalatka (Palatca), as well as certain scattered villages elsewhere. Some of the Transylvanian Hungarians from the villages around Brassó (Braşov) and beside Déva (Deva) are nicknamed 'Csángó'.

In Transylvania most garments for men are made, even today, out of materials grown and raised at home, out of cloth from the wool of their own sheep. For that reason the basic colour remains a natural greyish-white or brown. The manufactured blue cloth suit which came into fashion at different times in the 19th century among Hungarians living elsewhere never became widespread in Transylvania.

Men wore their hair long in the last century, and in some places it was made into three plaits.

The high cap, which had gone out of fashion elsewhere, was still worn in Transylvania at the end of the last century, in the region of Kalotaszeg and in Szakadát (Săcădate) in the central part of Transylvania. The broad brimmed hat, which followed the high cap, came into fashion later in Transylvania and was fashionable longer. The Hungarians living in Moldavia wore it up to 1935. In summertime a straw hat was worn for work and in the winter a fur-cap made of black or white lamb.

The shirt was made out of hemp-linen, and later out of manufactured cambric. It had no collar or cuffs in the last century and the sleeves were wide. Collar and cuffs were introduced into the territory of Transylvania only in this century. Nowadays the short shirt is seen almost everywhere, but in the 19th century a long shirt was worn in the southern and eastern regions, in Torockó, among the Székelys of Lövéte (Lucta) and the 'Csángó' Hungarians around Brassó (Braşov). In the summer men wore the long shirt outside the trousers, but in the winter it was tucked in.

A kerchief on the neck and a wide leather belt had to be worn with the old type of shirt. The kerchief was usually black, and in Magyarpalatka it was also used for Sundays. A white tie, a fashion still older, is mentioned in a description of the costumes from 1794.

The wide leather belt was used as a pouch, where the man kept his money and his smaller tools. In Torockó and in the Aranyos district the belt was made of red leather.

In Transylvania the pantaloons, 'gatya', made of homespun linen are usually very narrow, but wide pantaloons are worn in a few places such as Kalotaszeg and Lozsád in the Hunyad district. The Kalotaszeg men used to go harvesting on the Great Plain, and some elements of the costume typical of the Plain spread among them. In winter tight breeches made out of grey or white homespun cloth were worn over the light pantaloons. The breeches have two slits in front with a flap in between, and are called 'harisnya', stockings. There is a red or black braid up the sides, and the breeches are held up by a long strap. They can still be seen today.

Breeches made out of homespun and home-woven cloth were still sewn by the man himself not so long ago. In Torockó the unmarried lad would wear breeches made out of grey frieze.

The 'Csángó' Hungarians of Moldavia wear tights, which, like the ones worn in Western Europe until the 15th century, consist of two separate legs, not sewn together.

In several parts of Transylvania, a linen jacket called 'friskó', is worn over the shirt for work.

The colour of the sheepskin vest is usually white and it is worn not only in the winter, but also for festive occasions. Sometimes it buttons at the side.

The sheepskin jacket or coat is shorter and reaches to the waist, a longer, more old-fashioned kind reaches to the knees. It is called 'ködmön' or 'kozsók', and is generally white with red decoration, if any. In Torockó and along the Aranyos river it has a fox-collar.

Short and long jackets and coats are made of grey, white or black homespun cloth or cloth made by artisans. In Magyarpalatka the man sewed not only his breeches himself, but also his jacket. Young men used grey cloth for their jackets, old men white. Many variations of these jackets, each with a different name, were known in Transylvania. In Kalotaszeg it is named 'condra' or 'daróc', and is usually white or brown, except for the one worn by the bride-groom, which is grey. If a man died he was dressed in his bridegroom's 'daróc'. Among the Székelys of the village of Lövéte the jacket is called 'zeke', and reaches to the ankles. It is grey for weekdays and black for Sundays. The people of Torockó bought the material for their 'condra' from the neighbouring Románians and dyed it black at home.

The 'szűr' or frieze-coat described in the previous chapters is not worn much in Transyl-vania, although it began to be used at the end of the last century in the district of Kalotaszeg, where it spread in place of the 'daróc'. It was made by the 'szűr'-tailors of Nagyvárad (Oradea), and was distinguished by a small upright collar. The black 'szűr' was considered a gentleman's 'szűr' in Kalotaszeg. White 'szűr' coats were made in Medgyes (Mediaş) and were worn in the nearby counties. In Magyarpalatka a sleeveless cape or hood was worn, the 'gluga'. As the 'szűr' and similar garments were made out of impregnated frieze, herdsmen sleeping outdoors on the snow would wrap themselves in it, over their sheepskin coat.

The 'guba' coat, is fairly rare in Transylvania. Along the river Szamos a grey 'guba' is worn. The one worn by the Hungarians of Central Transylvania is made out of plain frieze, has a hood, and is of knee length. Both the 'szűr' and the 'guba' are usually worn thrown over the shoulders, the sleeves hanging loose.

These garments are tailored along straight lines, and are grey, white or occasionally black. If there is any decoration, it is red. The colour grey may have come down from the medieval grey peasant clothing, whilst the white and especially the black woollen cloth and frieze sug-gest a more specialized mode of sheep-raising and wool-making.

Blue cloth hardly reached Transylvania although one or two garments—a vest, a jacket—made of it were worn in a few places, such as Torockó, Kalotaszeg, Szilágyság (Sălaj). A blue cloth jacket, named 'bujka', was very popular in the villages of Kalotaszeg, and similar ones were worn in Torockó and Alsó-Fehér county (Judeţul Alba). Among the Székelys of Udvarhely county (Judeţul Odorheiu) the cloth jacket was black.

A blue vest was worn by the Székelys living along the river Aranyos in Torockó and in the Mezőség (Cîmpia Ardealului). The 'Csángó' Hungarians living close to Déva wore a black vest. In the county Udvarhely not only the jacket but also the vest was black. However, the garments made of blue flannel or manufactured cloth were not known among the poorer and more isolated groups of Transylvania.

The blue breeches, which were worn all over Hungary during the last century, did not reach Transylvania except for the Szilágyság. Nor did the blue cloth pelisse—the 'mente'—ever come into fashion here.

Men's costumes in Transylvania could be distinguished from the rest of Hungarian costumes as they were made out of grey, white or brown frieze and homespun cloth. Manufactured blue-dyed cloth, popular elsewhere, never came into fashion among the Transylvanians. Laced sandals were more common in Transylvania than in other parts of the country.

At first men wore boots only on Sundays, but later boots were worn on weekdays as well. They used to have the seam at the side, but since the last century the seam has been sewn at the back. In Torockó and among the Székelys living along the river Aranyos the black Cordwain boots were adorned at the top with a blue silk cord and tassels. Similar boots were worn in the Uplands at the turn of the century. In Torockó the boots had three folds, and a typical and very Turkish detail of old Transylvanian boots was the heart-shaped patch

Székely bonnet, 1940

at the front. For weekdays laced boots were often worn. There was a kind of low boot worn by the Székelys which was laced at the inner or outer side. It was named 'cepők'.

The Transylvanian women parted their hair in the middle, reminiscent of Renaissance hairdressing. The Biedermeyer fashion of parting the hair in a T-shape never reached Transylvania.

The 'párta' of young girls remained in fashion far longer in Transylvania than among Hungarians elsewhere. Among the 'Csángó' Hungarians of Déva the bride had a red 'párta' even at the turn of the century, as black had not come into fashion here yet. In the district of Aranyosszék, a golden 'párta' was worn, and the 'Csángó' people living around Brassó also had a golden or a silver 'párta'. In Central Transylvania, in the Mezőség this headdress for young girls died out early but it long remained fashionable in the villages of Kalotaszeg.

In Moldavia, the Hungarian women and girls living in the villages along the river Beszterce (Bistriţa) had a way of combing their hair similar to the 17th century fashion of rolling the hair on a small wooden hoop. In the district of Kalotaszeg and Torockó a ring made of bone or copper was used, and the Székely women wore a tiny ring on their bun.

The married women's black frilled bonnet, the 'csepesz', is most typical, and is similar to the fashionable Biedermeyer bonnet.

Two or three strings of beads, usually red, but sometimes white or black are worn.

The homespun linen worn by the women is still embellished with woven patterns or embroidery similar to woven designs. The folds of the shift may be smocked in front, as in the Mezőség and Alsó-Fehér county. The 'Csángó' women around Brassó had very long shifts at the beginning of the century and collar and cuffs embroidered in gold.

The Renaissance shifts were gradually replaced by chemises with sleeves, and various kinds of blouses. The chemise is worn under the blouse, whilst the Renaissance shift was worn alone, not as underwear.

The skirt kept its older form in Transylvania. It did not get shorter, and only became broader in Kalotaszeg, but even there only moderately. A kind of kilt-like skirt is still worn by the women of Transylvania. It is a striped piece of woollen cloth which is wrapped around the waist, opening in front, and tied with a long narrow woven band. The 'Csángó' Hungarians of the Gyimes Pass (Ghimeş) tuck the left corner into the waist leaving the long white shift to show. No apron is worn with this type of skirt.

A similar type of skirt is the 'muszuj' or 'bagazia' worn in Kalotaszeg which will be discussed later.

Among the Székelys a skirt sewn of homespun woollen material with vertical stripes in red and blue, or red and black is very popular, and is called 'rokolya' or 'fersing'. In Alsó-Fehér county it was pleated so that the red stripes showed when the woman was young, and the blue ones when she was old. The bottom of the skirt was trimmed with a band of green or blue cotton or cloth. The 'Csángó' women wear their skirt sewn to the bodice. In some places, such as Szovát in the Mezőség, the skirt is tucked into a belt so that the petticoat becomes visible on both sides.

A white, finely pleated skirt is known among the Hungarians in most parts of Transylvania: in Kalotaszeg and Torockó, and in the Mezőség among the Székely and the 'Csángó' women around Brassó (Braşov). More modern skirts are not pleated as closely, but are gathered into larger flat folds and decorated at the bottom with several rows of ribbon.

Various kinds of bodices are worn over the shift, and more recently a kind of blouse has also come into fashion.

An interesting garment belonging to the Kalotaszeg costume is the fur-lined vest decorated with lace. Sheepskin coats are also worn. These are usually hip length, but among the 'Csángó' Hungarians of Déva they reach almost to the ground. The 'condra' or 'daróc' made of frieze was worn by both men and women.

According to contemporary descriptions, laced sandals were generally worn for work. These were replaced by boots with the seam at the side, and were red for young people. These boots often have a heart-shaped patch in front. Nowadays women's boots are mostly black.

Some of the splendid, colourful and harmonious costumes in Transylvania are those of the people of Kalotaszeg. The main occupations of the villagers are agriculture and animal-husbandry, and more recently woodcarving, masonry and railway-work. Their costumes are extremely traditional and conservative.

Young girls used to part their hair in the middle but recently they simply comb it back, parting it only in front of the 'párta'.

Whilst the fashion of the 'párta' has passed away in most places, in the villages of Kalotaszeg it is still worn on great holidays. The 'párta' is a paper hoop lined with red or blue and covered with pearls of various shades. Coloured ribbons reaching to the waist, hang down the back. On workdays the girls wear patterned kerchiefs on their heads, tied at the nape. On Sundays and lesser holidays the kerchiefs are tied below the chin.

Married women in Kalotaszeg used to roll their hair on a ring, covering it with a net and placing a band with lace and beads on their foreheads. The young married woman used to wear a big white tulle veil for a few years after her wedding. The corners were embroidered with coloured crewel. It is called a 'dulándle' (from 'tulle d'Anglais'). This big white veil was still worn in the years before the First World War, though among other groups of Hungarians this custom had died out earlier.

On great holidays, girls hang a tassel made of beads round their necks as well as ribbons hanging down their backs.

Besides the Renaissance type of shift a newer kind of chemise is also worn in the village of Kalotaszeg, with the sleeves sewn to the shoulder. At the end of the last century this type of chemise had narrow sleeves which came down below the elbow. The shift was embroidered either below the shoulder or along the sleeves, narrowing below the elbow; a similar one may be found in the dress of Transylvanian ladies in the 17th century, and still earlier in the late Gothic, or early Renaissance costume of Western Europe. The more recent chemise has either narrow or wide sleeves, and may be regarded as underwear, worn under the more novel blouses.

Both the shift and the petticoat are made of a special kind of linen in Kalotaszeg called frilled linen. It is beaten in water to give the surface a wrinkled effect.

The fur-lined vest, mentioned earlier, was closed at the side. It was made out of green or red cloth and was decorated with black crocheted lace.

The linen petticoat, 'pendely', was gathered into tiny pleats. On holidays as many as three petticoats were worn (especially by thin women, who wanted to look stouter), as well as two or three underskirts.

Skirts are long in Kalotaszeg. Two typical kinds of skirt may be seen here. One is the 'muszuj' or 'bagazia' already mentioned. This skirt is not sewn together in front and is fashioned out of black or dark blue satin or cotton: it is very wide and is gathered into fine pleats, which are smocked at the top. The bottom of the 'muszuj' is lined with a wide cloth band (or, more recently, a velvet band) of red or orange, or—for old women—dark green, claret or black. Later on these bands were embroidered. The two bottom corners of the 'muszuj' are tucked into the waist, so the coloured band is displayed, and a bit of the white petticoat can be seen on both sides. Whilst the 'Csángó' type of kilt-skirt is worn without an apron, the Kalotaszeg wide 'muszuj' is always worn with an apron.

Another kind of skirt worn in Kalotaszeg is sewn out of fine factory-made linen and, like the 'muszuj', is gathered into tiny folds. It is usually worn only by young girls, but in some place, by young women too. The newer kinds of coloured skirt are gathered into larger folds and are decorated at the bottom with several coloured bands.

The apron is also smocked at the top, and the smocking forms a pattern called 'darázsolás', i.e. 'wasping'. Silk or satin aprons are worn with the newer kinds of skirts, and are colourful and very elaborate for young people, darker and simpler for the older ones.

On great holidays, when girls put on their 'párta', a kerchief is spread over their arms with a flowered design on a green or white background.

The sheepskin vest worn by women used to be longer, but later became shorter and lavishly embroidered.

According to contemporary descriptions the women of Kalotaszeg used to wear the sheepskin coat called 'kozsók', which reached to the hip and was sparingly embroidered with silk. Later girls also wore a 'kozsók' but theirs was trimmed with white fur.

A kind of frieze-coat called 'condra' or 'daróc' was worn by the women. Young women's were white, older women's grey or brown. It reached below the waist and had a standing collar. The seams on the side were decorated with shreds of black or coloured cloth. At the turn of the century, this kind of coat was replaced by the shorter 'bujka', a straight jacket made out of dark blue wool or flannel, the Sunday 'bujka' decorated with rows of beads.

Laced sandals were also worn by the Kalotaszeg women, and today they sometimes wear them for work. Boots came into fashion in the last century, red for the young and black for the old. Today boots are usually black, but red are still occasionally worn in one or two villages.

The white, red and blue costumes of Torockó and the neighbouring Torockószentgyörgy (Colţeşti) are most picturesque. The inhabitants of Torockó used to mine iron ore, and were somewhat better of than the more conservative farmers of Torockószentgyörgy.

Women and girls part their hair in the middle. Young girls wear the festive 'párta', which is decorated with golden lace, originally only one row, but now three. The 'párta' is covered with black velvet and lined with red cotton. Light-coloured kerchiefs are worn by young girls, too.

Married women plait their hair in two braids which are then knotted and a copper ring is placed around the knot. Their coif is embroidered in white on black silk and is decorated with black or coloured ribbons and a row of lace. Ribbons hang down from the coif at the sides and back. For one or two years after their wedding young women wear a white shawl-like veil. This veil was worn in the way that Hungarian ladies of the 17th and 18th centuries wore theirs: wound around the chin, gathered into folds on both sides of the forehead, and fastened on each side with three pins. The two ends of this shawl are embroidered and trimmed with lace. On weekdays women wear a kerchief which is tied at the nape in warm weather, but in cold weather and for going to church, it is tied under the chin.

Three or four strings of beads are worn around the neck.

In Torockó the shift is similar to the Kalotaszeg shift, and today is made of manufactured linen. The needlework on the collar and cuffs is red for young girls and blue for married women. Another kind of shift has needlework not only on the collar and cuffs, but also down the front and on the sleeves at the shoulder. Young girls used to wear an extra narrow cuff on this shift, which was known as 'sleeve-like-a-pipe'. In Kalotaszeg this cuff went out of fashion much earlier than in Torockó.

At the beginning of this century a shift was worn decorated with tiny copper spangles on the shoulder, sleeves and cuffs. This 'spangled shift' could only be worn by young married women for one or two years after their wedding. The 'spangled shift' is also mentioned in descriptions of the noblewomen's wardrobe in the 17th century.

A bodice was worn over the shift and over that a straight flannel jacket, without a collar buttoning in front. Today it has gone out of fashion and young people wear blouses and knitted jackets, whilst older women put on warm shawls.

The inner petticoat was sewn to the shift, until quite recently. The shift has now become short and is worn with two or three petticoats.

Two kinds of skirts may be distinguished in Torockó. One is similar to the 'muszuj', but it is tucked up only on weekdays, and is unlined. Young girls and young married women have a skirt, 'fersing', made of fine white linen with very close pleats, and worn only for the most festive occasions. It is sewn to the bodice, 'kösnyő', which is held together with a small embroidered flap, the rectangle 'fűzdő'. Under this little flap is a vertical band with red or black lace. All this is girded with a belt made of cords, again reminding one of the costumes of the nobility in the 17th century, the age of the Turkish occupation of Hungary.

A velvet apron matched the 'muszuj', but the white 'fersing' was worn as green cloth apron decorated with lace. Recently the aprons have been made out of thinner materials.

For the upper garment, a sleeveless vest called 'bunda' is worn. It is made of white sheepskin, straight at the waist, and has a standing fox collar. It is worn thrown over the shoulders. It is not thought fit for very old women to wear a 'bunda'.

Young girls and women who still wear the 'párta' have a pleated cape for church, made of dark blue or black cloth and reaching a little below the waist.

A 'pelisse' or 'mente' is also worn by the women of Torockó. It is made of dark blue or black cloth, flaring at the bottom, and is trimmed with white sheepskin two or three inches wide, and decorated with braiding.

The vest is made of green cloth or, more recently, of green silk, and is lined with lambskin.

On Sundays the women put on red boots, which reached above the knee, the soft leather being wrinkled into 15–20 folds. Knitted woollen stockings were worn with them; red-and-white striped ones for young people, blue-and-white striped for older people. Today only the bride wears red boots, otherwise the boots are black and the top is no longer wrinkled.

The Székelys form the major group of Hungarians in Transylvania. The village of Lövéte is especially traditional in its dress, and this will be taken as representative of Székely costume.

Women parted their hair in the middle. Young girls plaited it in one braid for Sundays and into two for weekdays, and fastened it up in a wreath. The 'párta' was only worn by the bride at her wedding, and at the ceremony of "knotting-up-the-hair" the 'párta' was placed on top of the knot of hair. After the wedding the young woman went to church in a kind of Biedermeyer bonnet, with a frill of starched black lace in front. A white shawl was tied over the black bonnet with one end across the chin. On Sundays women wore kerchiefs tied under the chin. In the summer a straw hat with a very wide brim was worn for working in the fields.

Three or four strings of red or black beads are worn around the neck. Up until the end of the First World War they wore black velvet ribbons around their necks as well.

The Renaissance shift was either never worn in Lövéte or went out of fashion very early. The shift here had a square-cut neckline and was made out of homespun linen. The ends of the sleeves were left open and embroidered with red yarn. This embroidery has gone out of fashion, and since the First World War the sleeves have ended in cuffs.

The inner petticoat is also made out of homespun linen and is rather narrow. Three or four wider petticoats are put over it.

The skirt named 'rokolya' is made of homespun linen too. Red is the favourite colour, but for Advent and Lent the skirt must be black or dark blue. The bride has a 'rokolya' of fine white cambric and should a young girl die, she is burried in this. The skirt—not to be confused with the 'rokolya'—is made out of dark blue cloth and is worn only in winter. The bottom is trimmed with two bands of black or green velvet, one narrow and one broad.

Formerly, the apron was also made out of homespun linen, but now it is sewn out of factory-made silk, often trimmed with lace. Aprons with black stripes at the bottom are also used.

The bodice is made out of red, green or blue silk with a broad band of black velvet at the bottom. The opening for the sleeves has a narrow black velvet border, and the neck a slightly broader one. The bodice is laced with black cord.

There is a white sleeveless fur vest called little 'bunda', which is very short, not reaching the waist. It is very low-cut in front and decorated with red leather.

In the winter, elderly women wear a cloth jacket reaching to the waist, without a collar or buttons, but tied at the neck.

Boots were formerly red and very pointed, with high heels. The toe of the boots is now rounded like those of Kalotaszeg, and is trimmed with a contrasting colour. In the summer, woollen slippers are worn. Shoes are becoming general here too.

THE PROCESS
OF ABANDONING PEASANT COSTUMES
('THE UNDRESSING')

Finally, the process and the reasons for discarding peasant costumes for the sake of urban fashion—or 'the undressing'—will be discussed.

In the course of the 19th century the financial situation of the peasants improved as the technical development of industry speeded up. This had a double influence on peasant culture.

On the one hand, the traditional costumes became more lavish, and more expensive materials were used, while on the other hand, it became possible to break away from the traditional limitations of peasant life with its rigid customs. The abandonment of peasant costumes began at about the same time when they had reached their height in the 19th century.

What is the essence of the process? As already pointed out, traditionalism did not mean independence from higher social classes or from urban culture. The influence, however, was a gradual process, the accepted elements always being adapted according to the aesthetics of peasant tradition. But when peasants abandoned their former costumes, they gave up the principle of peasant tradition.

Regarding the materials used, the process meant that homespun materials were completely disregarded and replaced by mass produced materials. The old type of tailoring along straight lines changed for curved lines of cut. Whilst peasant costumes in their prime were most colourful and pure colours were worn together, the change meant that the colour-scheme became narrower and more monotonous. Fewer garments were worn together. Fashion changed rapidly. The close relationship of the man or woman with their costumes became looser.

Men abandoned their costumes sooner than women. Many peasants had to seek labour in town and they did not like to look conspicuous in their clothing. One of the main motives for women abandoning their costumes was that the weight of the many skirts worn one over the other is far from practical. Women who were ill were often the first to stop wearing the traditional clothing. Children were the next to be dressed in town fashions, followed by young girls, and then by young women.

The process had a sequence according to pieces of garments. It usually began with footwear and ended with the fashion of hair and headwear. One may often see women in traditional costume with fashionable urban shoes or sandals on their feet. Peasant women who have completely abandoned their costume often still stick to their former knot of hair and coif, as was often to be seen not long ago in Mezőkövesd.

Peasants who have abandoned their costumes may still be bound to former customs of clothing in certain traits. The process is not simple, it is not easy to change from one principle of clothing to another.

The traditions of peasant life demanded that a marriageable young girl had enough clothing for a lifetime. This principle has remained: a young woman endeavours to have enough town dresses to last her a lifetime, or at least very many years, and has many more clothes than is customary in town.

At the present stage of the process, which seems to be the final one, the urban garments are mostly no longer made by the peasants themselves nor by artisans, who always modified the fashion a bit, but are bought ready-made. Buying ready-made clothes means that the chance to adaptation has been given up completely. But although this is no longer possible, the stubborn peasant taste still persists at least in combining garments and colours which do not seem suitable to urban taste. In this way there is still a difference between the clothing of peasants and urban fashions.

SUMMARY

Peasant costumes developed as a result of various economic, cultural and social circumstances in the 19th century. What the richest period of costumes meant in material, cut, colour and decoration has been described, as well as the process which brought about the decline of the traditional costumes, and their merging into urban clothing.

Analysis shows that three factors played a role in the formation of Hungarian peasant costumes: 1) The clothing of higher classes of society in different historical periods; 2) influences from both the East and the West; 3) the imaginative ideas of the peasants themselves.

As the economic, cultural and social situation of the peasant was different from that of the higher social classes, this meant a difference in the aesthetical-psychological traits manifested in peasant attire. Of the influences that reached them, the peasants accepted certain ones and rejected others, adapting certain garments, whilst others—which were felt to be foreign— were never adopted.

Peasants reacted in a most positive manner to certain forms, and it was this which became the basis of peasant costumes in their prime: the shift of Renaissance origin, the linen petticoat, parting the hair in a T-shape, the sheepskin jacket, red or black boots with seams at the side and the soles turned inside-out from the era of the Turkish occupation. The constant features in men's costume are: the shirt cut in eastern fashion with open sleeves and no collar, the wide, gathered linen 'gatya', the frieze-coat or 'szűr', the sheepskin cloak and sheepskin jacket, the neck-scarf coming from the 18th-century western fashion, and laced sandals and boots almost the same as those worn by women. Variations of these basic forms are found all over the country, giving the impression that they are timeless elements of Hungarian costume. The material derives from agriculture and animal husbandry.

Other garments belonged for a shorter time to 'classical' peasant costumes, i.e. peasant costumes in their prime, and at a different period in different parts of the country. Such elements of dress are the headwear for both men and women, the upper garments, and the various skirts and breeches. A variety of these garments followed each other, but the linen shirt, shift, petticoat and 'gatya' remained fairly unchanged. The upper garments were mostly made by artisans or by industry. They were rarely made at home. They are tailored along curved lines of cut. The differences in costumes in various regions may be distinguished especially by the headwear and the upper garments.

Costumes reached their prime at different times in different regions, and the length of time each garment was fashionable also varied. The suit made of white frieze, for instance, had disappeared in the Great Plain by the end of the 18th century, while in the Uplands it was still mentioned in the 19th century, and in Transylvania it is still worn today.

The peasants in different territories of the country were influenced by higher society in different ways. For instance, the blue cloth suit was already accepted by the wealthier peasants of northwestern Transdanubia and the agrarian towns of the Great Plain at the beginning of the 19th century, when the lesser nobility were still wearing this kind of suits themselves. In other places it spread much later. The peasants of the Sárköz began wearing blue cloth only in the 19th century after the liberation of the serfs; the 'Palóc' people only around 1890; and the Hungarians of Slavonia only in 1910, when this kind of suit had long disappeared from the wardrobe of the higher classes. And the fashion of blue cloth hardly reached Transylvania, at all.

The coif with golden lace disappeared from the town of Kecskemét in the Great Plain at the end of the 18th century. In other parts of the Great Plain and among the 'Jász' people it was still mentioned in the 19th century, and among the 'Palóc' it is only now beginning to disappear.

The Gothic style of pinning up the skirt on one or both sides was revived in the urban style of the 18th century. This fashion occurs in Hungarian costumes in regions very far from one another: in Transdanubia in the Sárköz, in Fadd, in Szenna, as well as among the Hungarian of the Uplands and of Transylvania. It had almost disappeared by the end of the 19th century, but in the village Kazár of the Uplands and in the region of Kalotaszeg in Transylvania it is still fashionable.

The similarity between the Hungarian costumes of different regions is due partly to the same basic forms of clothes. Another reason is that the economic, social and cultural circumstances of the 19th century had the same effect on the peasantry everywhere in Hungary. The costumes, which reached their prime at a different period in various places, all went through similar stages of development. For instance, the way the colour-scheme developed the similar preference of colours, the tendency towards a rhythm of colour, the habit of wearing many skirts, the endeavour to broaden the waist, the accumulation of material and ornament, the stiffening of forms and decorations, all these are consequences of a similar peasant attitude towards costume.

In the past few decades the life of Hungarian peasants has radically changed. Peasants are becoming integrated into Hungarian society as a whole. A separate popular culture has ceased to exist and with it, one of the forms of expression of peasant aesthetics will also gradually disappear: peasant costumes.

BIBLIOGRAPHY

General works

Bikkessy, Joseph Heinbacher Edler von: *Pannoniens Bewohner in ihren volkstümliche Trachten*, Wien, 1820.

Jaschke, Franz: *National-Kleidertrachten und Ansichten von Ungarn*, Wien, 1821.

Vahot, I.: *Magyarföld és Népei* (The Land of the Magyars and Its People), Pest, 1846.

Valerio, T.: *Costumes de la Hongrie et des Provinces Danubiennes*, Paris.

Kubinyi, F.—Vahot, I.: *Magyarország és Erdély képekben* (Hungary and Transylvania in Pictures), Pest, 1855.

Malonyai, D.: *A magyar nép művészete* (The Art of the Hungarian People) I–V. Budapest, 1907–1922.

Garay, Á.: "Régi magyar férfihajviseletek" (Old Ways of Dressing Men's Hair), *Néprajzi Értesítő*, 1911.

Bátky, S.—Győrffy, É.: *L'Art populaire hongrois*. Introduction par Ch. Viski. Budapest, 1928.

Győrffy, I.: *A cifraszűr* (The Embroidered 'Szűr' or Frieze-Coat), Budapest, 1930.

Palotay, G.: "A magyarországi női ingek egy szabástípusa" (A Type of Hungarian Shift and its Cut), *Néprajzi Értesítő*, 1931, 1938.

Kerékgyártó-Ujvári, A.: *A magyar női haj- és fejviselet* (Hairdressing and Headwear of Hungarian Women), Budapest, 1937.

Palotay, G.—Konecsni, A.: *Magyar népviseletek* (Hungarian Folk Costumes), Budapest, 1938.

Győrffy, I.: *A magyarság néprajza. I. Viselet* (The Ethnography of the Hungarians. I. Costumes), Budapest, 1941.

Ortutay, Gy.: *A magyar nép művészete* (The Art of the Hungarian People), Budapest, 1941.

Kresz, M.: *Magyar parasztviselet 1820–1867* (Hungarian Peasant Costumes) Budapest, 1956.

Fél, E.—Hofer, T.—Csilléry, K.: *L'Art populaire en Hongrie, Ungarische Bauernkunst, Hungarian Peasant Art*, Budapest, 1958.

Fél, E.: *Népviseletek* (Popular Costumes), Budapest, 1962.

The Great Plain

Ecsedi, I.: "A hortobágyi pásztorviselet" (The Costumes of the Herdsmen in the Hortobágy), *Néprajzi Értesítő*, 1914.

Papp, L.: "A kecskeméti viselet múltja" (The Costumes of Kecskemét in the Past), *Néprajzi Értesítő*, 1930.

Győrffy, I.: "A nagykun viselet a XVIII. században" (The Costumes in Great Cumania in the 18th Century), *Ethnographia*, 1937.

Zoltai, L.: "A debreceni viselet a XVI–XVIII. században" (The Costumes in Debrecen in the 16th–18th Centuries), *Ethnographia*, 1938.

Transdanubia

Kodolányi, J.: *Ormánság*, Budapest, 1960.

Dömötör, S.: *Őrség*, Budapest, 1960.

Kalota, L.: *Sárköz*, Budapest, 1962.

Vajkai, A.: *Balatonmellék* (The Region of the Balaton), Budapest, 1964.

The Uplands

Palotay, G.: "Egy nógrádmegyei falu ruházata" (The Clothing of a Village in Nógrád County), *Néprajzi Értesítő*, 1930.

Fél, E.: "A ruházkodás Martoson" (Women's Clothing in Martos), *Néprajzi Értesítő*, 1942.

Győrffy, I.: *Matyó népviselet* (The Costumes of the Matyó People), Budapest, 1956.

Transylvania

Haáz, F. R.: *Lővéte. Emlékkönyv a Székely Nemzeti Múzeum 50 éves jubielumára*, (Volume in Honour of the 50th Anniversary of the National Székely Mǔseum), 1931

Tőkés, B.: "A mezőségi magyar viselet" (The Hungarian Costumes in the Mezőség), *Néprajzi Értesítő*, 1935.

Nagy, J.: *A kalotaszegi magyar népi öltözet* (The Hungarian Popular Clothing in Kalotaszeg), Bucureşti, no date.

Nagy, J.: *A torockói magyar népi öltözet* (The Hungarian Popular Clothing in Torockó), Bucureşti, no date.

PLATES

I Girls and boys from Kalocsa in peasant costume, 1967

II Embroidered bodice from Szakmár, 1940.
Ethnographical Museum, Budapest

III Girls from Sióagárd, 1967

IV Young woman from Kapuvár, around 1950

V Boy from Kapuvár, around 1930

VI Collar of beads from Sárköz, around 1910. Ethnographical Museum, Budapest

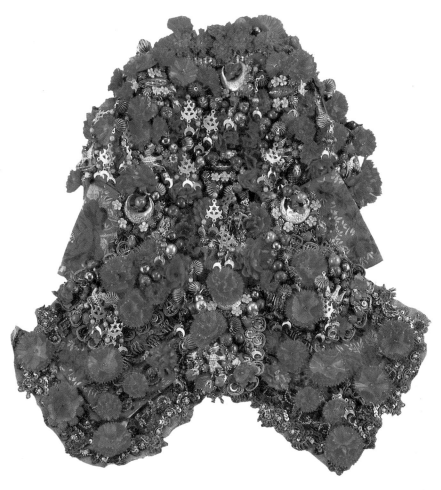

VII Coif from Püspökbogád, around 1900. Ethnographical Museum, Budapest

VIII Embroidery on the end of the veil
worn by young women,
Sárköz district, end of 19th century.
Ethnographical Museum, Budapest

IX Dressing the bride,
Hollókő, 1967

X Bride from Boldog, 1967

XI Young couple and a woman
from Kazár, 1967

XIII Married women
from Mezőkövesd,
around 1050

XII Young girls from Buják, 1967

XIV Coif from Martos,
around 1900

XV Kalotaszeg women dressed
for Good Friday, 1967

1 Girls from Kalocsa, 1967

XVI Young woman wearing veil, district
of Kalotaszeg, beginning of 20th centur

2 Detail of an embroidered
frieze-coat or, 'szűr',
Kisújszállás, end of 19th century

3 Man wearing an embroidered
frieze-coat, or 'szűr'
from the Hortobágy Puszta,
around 1930

4 Detail of an embroidered sheepskin cloak,
or 'suba' from the Jászság district, end of 19th century.
Ethnographical Museum, Budapest

5 Short sheepskin cloak
from the Hajdúság district, Derecske,
beginning of 20th century.
Ethnographical Museum, Budapest

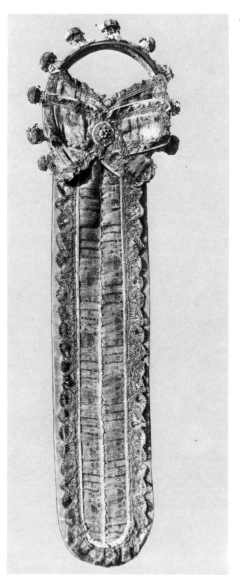

6 Pearl wreath for young girls, Hajdúság, around 1870. Ethnographical Museum, Budapest

7 Detail of a coif from the Sárköz district. Ethnographical Museum, Budapest

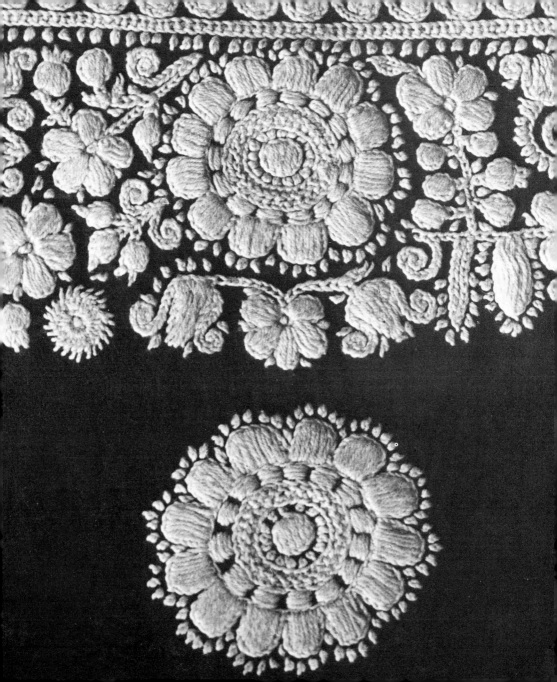

9 Girls and boys from Sárpilis, 1967

8 Old woman from Decs, Sárköz district, 1967

10 Women from Sióagárd, 1967

11 White mourning from Csököly, 1926

12 Mother and child
from Hollókő, 1967

13 Young woman
from Kapuvár, 1967

14 Young woman
from Kazár, 1967

15 Woman
from Kazár, 1967

16 Young woman
from Galgamácsa, 1967

17 Old woman
from Kazár, 1967

18 Woman
from Mezőkövesd,
beginning
of 20th century

19 Woman wearing
a sheepskin jacket,
from Mezőkövesd,
beginning
of 20th century

20 Girl and
young woman
from Boldog, 1936

21 Little girl
from Boldog,
around 1930

22 Girls from Buják, 1967

23 Bride from Boldog, 1965

24 Girl wearing
a pearl wreath
from Kőrösfő, 1960

25 Pearl wreath
from the district
of Kalotaszeg,
Kalotaszentkirály, 1960

26 Woman
from the district
of Kalotaszeg, 1962

27 Girl from the district
of Kalotaszeg
in a straw hat, 1962

28 Smocked shift
from Torockó (Rimetea),
beginning of the 20th
century.
Ethnographical
Museum, Budapest

29 Girls from Torockó
(Rimetea), 1960

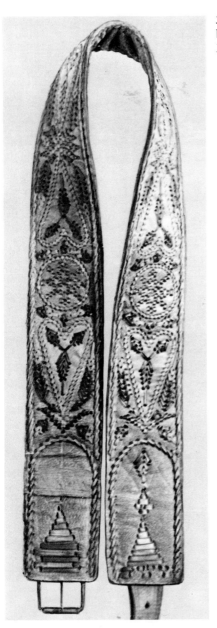

30 Wide belt from Torockó (Rimetea),
beginning of 20th century.
Ethnographical Museum, Budapest

31 Man from Magyarvalkó, 1967

32 Székely men, Csíkszentmárton, 1967